ASK THE BUTTERFLIES

ASK THE BUTTERFLIES

New and Selected Poems

Beverley Rose Enright

Copyright © 2019 by Beverley Rose Enright.

Library of Congress Control Number:		2019917308
ISBN:	Hardcover	978-1-7960-6790-3
	Softcover	978-1-7960-6789-7
	eBook	978-1-7960-6788-0

All rights reserved. No part of this book may be reproduced or transmitted in any form or by any means, electronic or mechanical, including photocopying, recording, or by any information storage and retrieval system, without permission in writing from the copyright owner.

Scripture quotations marked NKJV are taken from the New King James Version. Copyright © 1982 by Thomas Nelson, Inc. Used by permission. All rights reserved.

Any people depicted in stock imagery provided by Getty Images are models, and such images are being used for illustrative purposes only.
Certain stock imagery © Getty Images.

Print information available on the last page.

Rev. date: 11/20/2019

To order additional copies of this book, contact:
Xlibris
1-888-795-4274
www.Xlibris.com
Orders@Xlibris.com
776616

CONTENTS

ENDANGERED

AT MUSTANG ISLAND BEACH 1
REMEMBERING THE SEASHORE 4
REMEMBERING SHEL SILVERSTEIN 6
WITH RESPECT TO POPEYE AND OLIVE OYL 7
I'M IN TEXAS 9
THE BALLAD OF ROSY RABBIT AND HAIRY HARE,
OR, WHO ARE THE BUNNIES? 10
THE WAY IT IS..20
ON THE DEATH OF TREES 21
FEBRUARY SPRING 35
"LESS IS MORE" 36
A CHRISTMAS CAROL, 2018 38
HOW TO MAKE A GREAT TOSSED SALAD 39
THE HOT SEXPOT 40
LINES AFTER READING RANDALL MANN'S POEM
"ORDER" 42
WHAT GOES AROUND 44
A FUGING TUNE..45
COUNTER VIEWPOINTS 46
A MAN WHO CAN USE HIS HANDS 47
GLOSA ON A POEM BY ALEX GILDZEN AS A
MEISTERLIEDE 48
OUR MARRIAGE IS A MUNDANE MIRACLE 51
YOU NEVER REALLY ARE DIVORCED 52
UNDEFINED 53
INTIMATIONS OF DIVINITY 54
ICON OF CHRIST IN GLORY 55

THE HOLY FACE 56
TO TED 58
THE "USELESS" FLOWERS 59
TO JUDY 60
IN A MINOR TURNING TO MAJOR KEY 61
TO PHILIP DACEY DYING OF LEUKEMIA 63
PHILIP DACEY MEETS WALT WHITMAN,
GERARD MANLEY HOPKINS, AND
THOMAS EAKINS IN HEAVEN 65
SWAN COTTAGE 67
THE GOLDEN SWAN 69
EARTHWORM 70
ENDANGERED 71
FRAGMENT OF SOLITUDE 74
TO A BUTTERFLY 75
GLOBAL WARNING 77
ASK THE BUTTERFLIES 78

SELECTIONS FROM SONNET SEQUENCES:

SONNETS 1 83
SONNET 2 86
SONNET 14 (ALSO 53) 87
SONNET 22 88
SONNET 23 89
SONNET 26 90
SONNET 29 92
SONNET 31 93
SONNET 36 94
SONNETS 42 95
SONNET 46 97
SONNET 55 98
SONNET 56 99
SONNET 58 100

SONNET 60	101
SONNET 71	102
SONNET 82	103
SONNET 89	104
SONNET 91	105
SONNET 96	106
SONNET 107	107
SONNET 123 BLUES	108
SONNET 126	109
SONNET 136	111
SONNET 137	112
SONNET 138	113
SONNET 139	114
SONNET 142	115
SONNET 146	116
SONNET 150	118
I. THE GIFT OF A TEXT FULL OF ERRORS	119
IV. THE REMOVABLE DISCONTINUITY	120
V. THE PINCHING THEOREM	121
VI. LEIBNIZ'S DERIVATIVE WITH RESPECT TO DESCARTES'S CROSS RELIGIOUSLY	122
VII. LEIBNIZ'S DERIVATIVE WITH RESPECT TO DESCARTES'S CROSS PHILOSOPHICALLY	123
VIII. RULES OF POWER, POLYNOMIAL, PRODUCT, AND QUOTIENT	124
X. IMPLICIT DIFFERENTIATION	125
XII. SET THE DERIVATIVE EQUAL TO ZERO TO GET THE MAX AND MIN	126
XXIV. THE MEAN VALUE THEOREM FOR INTEGRALS	127
XXVI. AREA BETWEEN TWO CURVES: WALKING ON WATER AT THE VOLO BOG	128
XXIX. THE SURFACE AREA OF WORLD WITHOUT END	129

XXXII. TRANSLATION PRINCIPLE AND FINDING THE SLOPE OF A LINE TANGENT TO A CURVE AT A POINT 130
XXXVI. CONTINUOUS FUNCTIONS 131
XXXVII. PROOFS OF THE LIMIT LAWS 132
XLI. THE NUPTIAL NIGHT OF THE COROLLARIES: CONSEQUENCES OF THE MEAN VALUE THEOREM 133
XLIII. THE CHAIN RULE 134
XLV. DERIVATIVES OF SINES AND COSINES 135
XLVI. ASYMPTOTES; INFINITE LOVE INCREASES WITHOUT BOUND AROUND THE WHEEL OF FAITH 136
L. ANTIDERATIVES 137
LII. RIEMANN SUMS AND THE INTEGRAL 138
LV. AREA BETWEEN TWO CURVES 139
LVI. VOLUME OF A SOLID OF REVOLUTION: DISK METHOD, OR EZEKIEL SAW THE WHEEL 140
LVII. VOLUME OF A SOLID OF REVOLUTION: SHELL METHOD, OR TED KOOSER'S "ONION WOMAN" REVISITED 141
LXVIII. DERIVATIVES AND INTEGRALS OF INVERSE TRIGONOMETRIC FUNCTIONS 142
LXXI. BASIC INTEGRATION FORMULAS: TED KOOSER'S "A CHILD'S GRAVE MARKER" 143
LXXVI. DIVERGENCE AND THE DEATH OF CETACEANS: OIL SPILL AT PRINCE WILLIAM SOUND ... 144
LXXVIII. INFINITE SERIES AS A CIRCLE BETWEEN TWO FACING MIRRORS 146
LXXIX. WHEN THERE'S NO ANTIDERIVATIVE FOR THE INTEGRAND F . . . AND THAT WORD WON'T DO EITHER 147
LXXXIX. FINDING MYSELF DUSTY ON DERIVATIVES ... 148
XCII. THE LOSS OF A PARTICULAR CONSTANT WHEN REVERSING: POWER RULE FOR DERIVATIVES AND ANTIDERIVATIVES 149

XCVI. THE SANDWICH THEOREM IN A SQUEEZING
PINCH BETWEEN A ROCK AND A HARD PLACE 150
XCVIII. THE BRIDGE LINKING DIFFERENTIATION
AND INTEGRATION: THE FUNDAMENTAL
THEOREM OF CALCULUS 151
C. BLOWING KISSES TO RON COLEMAN AT THE
KELVYN PARK HIGH SCHOOL RETIREMENT
DINNER JUNE 2008 152

IN THE LAND OF THE EXTINCT BIRDS

IN THE LAND OF THE EXTINCT BIRDS 157
ELEGY TO THE ELEPHANT BIRD 158
MEMORIUM TO THE MOA 161
A DIRGE FOR THE DODO.. 163
RONDEL FOR THE MAURITIUS RED HEN 166
RHONDEAU FOR THE RODRIGUEZ SOLITAIRE................ 167
PANTOUM FOR THE PIGEON HOLLANDAISE 168
SESTINA FOR THE STEPHENS ISLAND WREN 169
RUBAIYAT FOR INDIA'S PINK-HEADED DUCK 172
LAMENT FOR THE LABRADOR DUCK................................ 173
VILLANELLE FOR THE PAINTED VULTURE 175
BLUES FOR BRACE'S EMERALD HUMMINGBIRD 176
HAIKU FOR THE RYUKYU KINGFISHER 177
HEROIC COUPLETS FOR THE HEATH HEN 178
A BALLAD FOR THE AMERICAN IVORY-BILLED
WOODPECKER 180
SEXTILLA FOR THE IMPERIAL WOODPECKER OF
THE MEXICAN SIERRA MADRE.. 182
DOUBLE FIVE* FOR THE DELALANDE'S COUCAL 183
A LIMERICK FOR THE LAUGHING OWL 184
FUGUE FOR FORSTER'S TANNA DOVE 186
SEGUIDILLA FOR THE SAINT KITTS PUERTO
RICAN BULLFINCH.. 188
RUBLIW* FOR THE MARQUESAS FRUIT DOVE................. 189

OCTAVA RIMA ODE ON THE
HAWAIIAN ISLANDS 'O'OS 190
PUSHKIN SONNET FOR THE LAYSAN MILLERBIRD 192
GOLDEN SECTION THIRTEENER FOR THE
GUADELOUPE AMAZON 193
A CHANT FOR THE CHATHAM ISLAND BELLBIRD
(MAKO MAKO) 194
BLACK CAULDRON ANTHEM FOR THE GREAT AUK 195
TWIN TRIOLETS FOR THE CAROLINA PARAKEET 197
CURTAL SONNET* FOR THE ESKIMO CURLEW 198
PASSING AWAY STANZA FOR THE
PASSENGER PIGEON 200
A PARABLE FOR THE PARADISE PARROT 201

TRIOLETS OF TENDERNESS

OUR NATIONAL SYMBOL WAS ALMOST LOST 205
MOTHER'S DAY AT LOMBARD'S LILACIA PARK 207
ARCHANGEL WITH THE GOLDEN HAIR 208
NUTMEG 209
YOUR HANDS 211
JUST TO HOLD YOUR HAND 212
WHAT A COMFORT WAS YOUR VOICE 213
WITHOUT YOUR GLASSES 214
"THE VOICE OF MY BELOVED, BEHOLD HE
COMETH LEAPING" 215
THE VOICE OF LEAVES 216
MISTER RIGHT 218

ROMANTIC FEELINGS AND FANTASIES

FOUR LIEDER BY PHILIP KOPLOW 221
SPRING BIRD BLUES 222
DANCING SONG 223

MY SONG WAS GONE	224
THE SEA OF LOVE	225
APPLES	226
THE ANGEL WITH THE FLAMING DART	227
THE PRINCE	228
THIS TOO WILL PASS	229
BREAKFAST	230
ONLY A FANTASY	231
FANCIFUL DIALOGUE FOR WHEN WE FIRST MEET	232
YOU COME TO ME IN THE NIGHT	233
TELEPATHY	234
WILD HORSES	235
YOUR FACE	236
PARADELLE* OF PAST LOVE	237
PARADELLE OF SPENT PASSION	238
RED GLASS	239
TRAIN WRECK	241
IT'S OVER	242
WETNESS	243
RAIN SONG	244
AT LAKE PORTAGE IN CENTRAL MICHIGAN	245
IF I WERE A BLOOMING LILAC BUSH	247
"I AM THE ROSE OF SHARON AND THE LILY OF THE VALLEY"	248
"THY LOVE IS BETTER THAN WINE"	250
"RISE UP, MY LOVE, MY FAIR ONE, AND COME AWAY"	251
"BE THOU LIKE A YOUNG HART UPON THE MOUNTAINS OF SPICES"	252

ENDANGERED

AT MUSTANG ISLAND BEACH

I waded in the water until the rushing waves
splashed above my thighs,
and my feet sank in the sand below
as if an undertow pulled me toward the sea.

I feared then I would fall and flail and drown,
and so I turned and trudged against
the squid like tug of a strong tide.
Reluctantly I struggled toward the shore.

I joined my daughter searching
the shoreline when the waves rolled back
for places where the little shells,
the multicolored shells were stacked.

Finding them, she would stoop, scoop
handfuls of sand and shells to see
their colors of red and turquoise blue
and brown and golden yellow hue.

Despite the Texas tropic sun the air was chilly,
and the whipping wind after cold water
caused me to snuggle my towel dried body
in a fleece wrap as I sat in a mesh folding chair.

The breeding black-headed laughing gulls
sang with the steady rumble of the water.
I sank into sad reveries of the dying sea
drinking carbon dioxide from the air,

causing the ocean's PH drop toward acid
that eats the calcium carbonate, starving shells,
killing coral and shellfish, as if the mercury
in tuna and the oil spills were not enough,

as if the deafening sonic booms deep in the water
driving the whales to swim for quiet somewhere,
as if the radioactive garbage and bomb testing,
as if the over fishing were not enough,

as if the Pacific Ocean's garbage patch of plastic
nine feet deep and twice the size of Texas,
as if the tons of plastic found in stomachs
of dead whales and sea turtles washed ashore,

as if, I watch the sunset dance its colors on the water,
and my daughter, her husband, and her in-laws
build a fire on the sand. The electric cars and solar panels
may come too late to save what once lived in the sea.

And the coral reefs and the many species living
in marine museums and public aquariums
will not be enough to repopulate a future cleaned up,
if cleaning up is even possible, vast barren sea.

It's all about money, for critters and people do not matter.
I will die before disaster, but my grandchildren,
and here they are asking me if I want to eat
a burger or a hot dog with beef that comes

from cattle farting methane, a greenhouse gas.
What has humanity's so-called great cities
and vast use of coal, gas, oil, and water, yes,
poisoned water, come to? Ask the seas.

Ask the oysters, ask the clams,
ask the butterflies, ask the bees,
ask the pelicans, ask the terns, oh,
and ask the Gulf of Mexico.

REMEMBERING THE SEASHORE

      for Richard Greene

My first visit with the Atlantic Ocean
was at a beach near Boston
when I was twenty with a youth
so wimpy he laid on the beach towel
watching me play in the surf.

It's true the day was chilly
and the water much much colder,
but he didn't even put a toe in.
That was our only date,
and I was grateful he was gone.

My second visit was at Rockport, Maine.
My husband and I dined on lobster by the beach
on brown paper with white paper cups
of melted butter. Those were the freshest
and cheapest lobsters we ever ate.

I took sea urchin, limpet, and clam shells
home to decorate my paintings; some I sold
and some were lost in moving.
The chairman of the philosophy department's wife,
Irena, took me to Assateague Island back then.

She wanted an epiphany and poetry,
but got miles of sand, prose, and empty sea.
As for me, applying sunblock, I missed my nose.
I filled a bucket with stones and shells; the shells
I glued to a huge painting of crashing waves.

I was pregnant then, and five years later
I took my son with another couple of children
to Virginia Beach and watched them play
in the sand and merrily wade in the water.
Maybe I did it too. I don't remember.

After we moved to Illinois we visited old friends
who had moved to Myrtle Beach. The shops
were full of elegant shells, all shapes and sizes
that we couldn't find on the shore among
the horseshoe crabs. So we bought some.

The crape myrtles were blooming everywhere
and the sea was warm and the summer sun
burned as the water washed away the sun screen.
Four decades passed before I with my grandchildren
walked into the Atlantic at the Gulf of Mexico.

REMEMBERING SHEL SILVERSTEIN

Oh, when I think of Sarah Stout
who would not throw the garbage out,
I ponder and I wonder where
does all those piles of garbage go?
Do they all go to make a hill
or fill up a humongous hole?
And do we have enough earth space
to hide away the toxic waste?
And as it all accumulates,
then how will that affect our fates
and those who follow us, and why
so many will get sick and die
so young as we crowd round the earth,
and what of life for what it's worth
will still survive?
It's all too sad to think about
except decrease what I throw out
and choose
to recycle and reuse,
to recycle and reuse.

WITH RESPECT TO POPEYE AND OLIVE OYL

> *giving the raspberry to John Ashbery's sestina "Farm Implements and Rutabagas in a Landscape" for its portrayal of beloved characters*

In the harbor rocks a houseboat as a strong
wind hints of a coming gale. Poopdeck Pappy eats
sardines as he sits holding a can of spinach
for a chaser. In between bites, he tells Popeye
seated beside him, tales of his days as a young sailor
in the merchant marine. "Toot – toot"

whistles Wimpy as he climbs aboard the houseboat. "Toot – toot",
he wrinkles up his nose at the strong
odor of the sardines. He tips his hat to the sailors.
"Would you have some other eats,
say a hamburger? I would gladly pay you Tuesday, Mr. Popeye"
Wimpy inquires politely, shuddering as he notices the spinach.

Pappy sneers as he holds out the can, "Have some spinach!"
Wimpy flutters his hand. "Toot – toot,
my dear Mr. Poopdeck and Mr. Popeye,
have you no hamburgers in that strong
icebox in the galley? You know I much prefer to eat
hamburgers. I do not desire to be a sailor."

As Wimpy descends to the galley, the old sailor
turns to open the can of spinach.
But before either Pappy or Popeye eats
any, a yacht pulls along side the houseboat. "Toot – toot."
A gussied up elderly lady is standing on deck, with a strong
resembulinks toos duh Sea Hag, thinks Popeye.

"Why hello, Poopdeck, my long lost lover, and Popeye,"
the old lady flirts in falsetto, smelling strangely strong
of rotting fish. "We meet again after all these years, my dear sailor,"
Sensuously shaped in whale bone covered with fish scales, she eyes
the spinach
uneaten through her veil of fine fishnet. "Toot – toot"
sounds from the galley where Wimpy burps and belches as he eats

the hamburgers from the icebox cooked over a fire in a can. He eats,
but Olive Oyl holding Swee'pea discovers him and calls, "O Popeye!"
She pulls the curious Swee'pea away, as Wimpy goes "toot – toot".
The disguised Sea Hag entreats. "O Poopy, come to my yacht, my
sailor!"
"I don't remembers yuh!" snaps Pappy. Popeye gulps the spinach,
rescues the houseboat, singing while the yacht sinks as the gale grows
strong:

"I'm strong toos duh finish, cuz I eats
me spinach. I'm Popeye,
duh sailor man." Toot – toot!

I'M IN TEXAS

in Texas
where the grackles cackle
and white winged doves
hoot like owls,

in Texas
where crape myrtle's fertile
and quaking geckos toss
then regrow tails,

in Texas
where rattlesnakes shake rattles
and fire ants inflame
fast up your pants,

in Texas
where the heat beats hotter
and raindrops evaporate
before they drop,

in Texas
where the floods flow deeper
and dainty deer dance
in the dark,

in Texas.

THE BALLAD OF ROSY RABBIT AND HAIRY HARE, OR, WHO ARE THE BUNNIES?

Hairy Hare was a rugged jackrabbit,
    And his strong legs could jump a horse.
Hairy Hare was a handsome jackrabbit,
    Long and lean and full of life force.

Rosy Rabbit was a soft round bunny,
    Plump and pretty as a clump of kale.
Rosy Rabbit was a pale gold honey,
    And no way was she up for sale.

Rosy Rabbit lived in a big high hutch
    Safe and secure from possums and cats.
Rosy Rabbit roomed with a female Dutch.
    The hounds kept out the rattlers and rats.

No coyotes or foxes could come near the place
    Because of those huge hunting hounds.
And a six foot fence surrounded that space
    And the large dogs patrolled round the grounds.

Rosy Rabbit was a cherished and pampered pet
    By the daughters and son of the man
Who owned the ranch with the strange silhouette
    Of a longhorn topped orangutan.

Dad was a different gentleman cowboy
    With a taste for the offbeat and odd.
He liked his steaks well seasoned with soy
    Sliced pancake-thin fried with cod.

His wife was gentle and quite sentimental,
    As delicate and sunny as a Texas rose,
As merry as a birthday and just as emotional,
    And fond of lacy ruffles and bows.

One day as Hairy was exploring the area,
    Jumping the cacti, out-hopping a fox,
He came to the ranch with the strange hacienda
    Curious at what looked so unorthodox.

Jumping the fence was great fun for Hairy
    And out-hopping the hounds just as much,
And he kept them in circles, baying and howling
    Till he spied Rosy caged with the Dutch.

Now jackrabbits mate with lady jackrabbits
    So they can get jackrabbit babies,
But they can't do the same with cottontail rabbits
    Or domestic rabbits, no bunnies.

Oh, they can get really up close and friendly,
    But the chromosomes just don't match up
Because they are three different species, you see,
    Cross-mating is sterile, screwed up.

But one look at Rosy and Hairy was caught
    With desire and longing for her,
And he knew from the strength of the feeling he got
    It was not going to pass but endure.

Hairy Hare hopped to the top of the cage
    And all the dogs barking brought out
Mom and Dad and the kids in a rage
    To see what the noise was about.

This was a signal for Hairy to leave
    And he whispered to her, "Later, dear"
And with several awesomely gigantic leaps
    He was gone, and they wanted to cheer.

Awestruck by his leaps and his handsome look,
    They wished one had grabbed a smartphone
To post pictures of him to brag on Facebook,
    And the kids wanted him for their own.

They got their wish in a surprising way
    Because Hairy came back to see Rosy.
They ran out the house when they heard the hounds bay,
    Silenced the dogs, and got nosy.

The boy took a picture before Hairy left.
    Now they knew why they'd see him again,
And they talked about fame, and crowds, and theft
    And what they should tell, how, and when.

Hairy came back there late in the night
    When he thought the hounds were asleep,
But one hound awoke and in the moonlight
    Saw Hairy who left in great leaps.

And so it went on; Hairy came and was gone.
    The dogs saw that no one did mind.
They were always hushed, could not even moan,
    And were told outright to be kind.

Rosy loved Hairy and how could she not
    Because he was handsome and strong,
But no matter how close and together they got
    Rosy knew something was wrong.

The family brought in a white male bunny
    Named Billy for Tulip the Dutch
So she wouldn't be sad without her own honey.
    Both rabbits moved to a new hutch.

Tulip got big and then had a litter
    Of five to delight all the kids.
They ignored Rosy and oh, that was bitter
    And into the corner she hid.

Rosy was happy when Hairy was near,
    But he was always coming and going.
And when Hairy asked her "What's wrong, my dear?"
    She said "babies" with her eyes overflowing.

Hairy knew inside him what was the matter
    And it was something he couldn't cure.
"No bunny blooms like my Rosy," he'd chatter.
    "No love was ever so pure."

But then he would leave. and Rosy would pine
    Not eat, and continue to droop.
The children took notice and saw her decline,
    And their playmates then started to snoop.

"It's that jackrabbit's fault, you silly dummies!
    You just let him come in and have her.
Now she can't have her very own bunnies,
    And there's nothing now that can save her."

Hairy was hurting, as Rosy kept pining,
    And the family tried to think what to do.
So they went to the vet to stop the kids whining.
    The vet had an idea or two.

He would find a male rabbit who looked like a hare
    From all the rabbit breeds that he knew
And put that rabbit's sperm in a syringe to stick where
    In Rosy the baby rabbits grew.

So Rosy got bigger and had her own litter
    With eight baby rabbits this time.
She was ecstatic, but Hairy got bitter
    And told her, "Not one of them's mine."

"But they're mine," Rosy said, "and I'm yours,
    So they're yours, and you must never forget,
That you don't always get the babies you want,
    You still want the babies you get."

None of her rabbits could hop like her Hairy
    But even jackrabbits could not,
And they didn't look at all like their Daddy
    But they favored their Mom, and that's that.

And that was good enough for good Hairy
    For they reminded him always of Rosy,
But his nature was wild-eyed and daring
    And he couldn't stay cuddly and cozy.

In the ranch house the family was talking
    About how to keep Hairy at home.
"It is always adventure he's stalking,
    and it's not safe to just let him roam."

"The time has come," said the rancher,
    "For us to make Hairy a star."
And he called in the builders and carpenters
    To make sets for Hairy's grand repertoire.

Oh, Hairy raced greyhounds and horses,
    Jumping high fences and towers
And crowds came hearing news from all sources,
    Cheered and filmed and even tossed flowers.

If there was a jackrabbit Olympics
    Hairy would take home the gold,
But every star athlete still always gets
    The prize of just growing old.

As the dogs and the horses got slower,
    Hairy still was a marvel to see.
As the heights of the bars were put lower,
    He still jumped with obvious glee.

And if anyone doubted the stories,
    The photos and films on TV,
And the internet documentaries
    Were proof of what Hairy could be.

Rosy was happy with only one litter
    Now that her Hairy stayed near,
And the family kept her rabbits with her
    And they had more rabbits each year.

But Billy and Tulip and their baby rabbits
    Were all sold or given away
To neighbors and friends so the family could visit
    And still pet and cuddle and play.

When the crowds continued to decrease
    And Hairy became last year's news,
The rancher decided that he would increase
    And vary the attractions they could choose.

He brought in some zebras and afghans
   For Hairy to race and jump over a gnu,
And (no surprise!) some orangutans
   And an ostrich to start a small zoo.

Rabbits live short intense lives fast
   And Hairy would need more than fuel
If he could continue to even hop past
   Ponies and collies and what then? A mule?

Rosy's babies and their babies and their babies too
   Were packing the pens and eating up feed,
Which was eating the profits, when only a few
   Pets were all his children would need.

Behind his wife's back, he spoke to the cook
   And a skinner who would keep it hush-hush
As they culled Rosy's offspring and covertly took
   The meat to chop up and to crush.

And in place of hot dogs and burgers for lunch
   To offer the people who came to his zoo,
There were nuggets and tenders and even a bunch
   Of deep fried rabbit corn dogs, but no rabbit stew.

The name of the meat was known but by a few.
   He neutered the males that remained in the pen.
And told each of his children to pick out one or two
   To still keep as pets, and what happened then?

Rosy and Hairy had a long chat
   Concerning their future, and was it a pot
Of boiling hot water or deep sizzling fat
   And how to escape that without getting caught.

Hairy could not jump the fence and take Rosy
    If he could still now leap that high.
But Rosy suggested as they cuddled up cozy,
    That they dig their way out on the sly.

That's what they did in a place that was hid
    Behind the garage and the shed.
Soon the tunnel was done and out they slid
    Before dawn and together they fled.

While outside the ranch was still much the same,
    And Hairy knew his own way around.
Rosy did not, and no one could blame
    Her for not recognizing the sound.

It was later that day when Hairy jumped away
    To scout for a safe place to sleep.
Rosy weary lay down becoming the prey
    Of a rattler who bit her foot deep.

Her piercing shriek made Hairy dash
    Back in a flash stomping and smashing the head
Of the snake, but his dear Rosy went fast,
    And whispering "my love", she was dead.

Oh, the pain of that loss as he lay down upon her
    And stroked her and licked her and cried,
"Rosy, my Rosy, O Death, please don't take her!"
    He tried to deny that she'd died.

"Well, then take me too!" and the sound of a shot
    From a rifle and a small piece of lead
Granted his wish when straightway it sought
    His heart, and he too was dead.

Off in the distance, a man and his son
   Started walking toward the place where they lay.
The man said to the boy who was holding the gun,
   "It didn't look like it was this far away.

That jackrabbit's bigger than I thought" as he stared
   "In fact, he's the biggest in size
I've ever seen except that famous hare,"
   And he stopped and wide opened his eyes.

"By God, it is Hairy! You shot Hairy Hare!
   Don't touch them. That's Rosy under him.
And look, there's a snake. Leave it there!
   Let it be. Pull out your smartphone, Jim.

Take pictures from every angle around them,
   Every close-up and detail too.
This is a bonanza, believe me, my son.
   Make sure you get each sort of view."

Now what comes next, he thought. *What's it be?*
   Let me think this out. Don't take them back
To orangutan man. They were trying to flee.
   "Put that smartphone away!" as he gave Jim a crack.

"But Dad, it's exciting, I want to show . . ." "NO!
   Once that's online, Jim, it's viral, and done.
A media swarm of gossips and liars . . . Oh!
   There's a hell hiding in Facebook, my son."

"We're going to put the corpses, also the snake
   In the pickup. You go get the truck.
And give me that smartphone so you will not make
   A mistake we can't take back, and we're stuck."

When the news and the photos went online, a crate
    Containing the remains and the digital pix
Was sent to a taxidermist who worked out of state
    Reconstructing the scene to the tiniest fix.

And it all came back to a new restaurant
    And was displayed behind sheets of glass,
And a gold sign with a black-lettered font
    Out in front told the name of the place.

THE RABBIT AND HARE, and inside on a wall
    Were pictures of Hairy in his glory days.
Menus were passed out that offered to all
    Many different hare and rabbit entrees.

But those stuffed figures proved to be very sad,
    And diners lost appetite for the fare.
So a change in the menus had to be made.
    Just a salad bar was now offered there.

It attracted the vegans, athletes, and folks
    On strict diets, and the tourists too.
No liquor was served, no coffee, no Cokes.
    It was a shrine to just dine and pitch woo.

Four security guards stood watch night and day.
    By the posters, cups, T-shirts, and statues in wood.
But thieves broke in and stole the stuffed lovers anyway
    Just like you suspected they would.

But their story and fate lives on in this song
    That tells us to live better and care
Despite all the cages, exploitations, and wrong,
    To love like Rosy and her Hairy Hare.

THE WAY IT IS

In this life, all kinds of things get broken,
and sometimes they can be fixed,
and sometimes they can't,
and if they can't,
sometimes they can be replaced,
and sometimes they can't be replaced.
What then?
This is what loss is all about.
What do you do when things get broken
and cannot be fixed or replaced?
Write poetry?

ON THE DEATH OF TREES

> *I think that I shall never see*
> *A poem lovely as a tree.*
>
> *A tree whose hungry mouth is prest*
> *Against the earth's sweet flowing breast;*
>
> *A tree that looks at God all day,*
> *And lifts her leafy arms to pray;*
>
> *A tree that may in Summer wear*
> *A nest of robins in her hair;*
>
> *Upon whose bosom snow has lain;*
> *And intimately lives with rain.*
>
> *Poems are made by fools like me,*
> *But only God can make a tree.*
>
> Joyce Kilmer, *"Trees"*

I think that I shall never see
any respect any more for this poem tattooed in my memory.
It was once found in every poetry anthology.
Now it is despised by the academic poetry police,
although it was ubiquitous as an oft-quoted masterpiece.
It's out of fashion like Longfellow whose lines still live because
passed down like nursery rhymes by grandparents and in-laws.
It's just too easy an example of butchered metaphor,
a jumble of body parts that don't connect what they stand for,
that don't correspond consistently between a person and a tree.
A mouth suckling the ground, eyes to the skies, free-

ly hirsute lifted arms that become a mass of hair adorned
with a bird nest, breast like Medusa's head unshorn
draped in cold white snow, and last of all, the rain
penetrates all female orifices, on top and underground, free rein.
Clichés, hackneyed phrases, banal piety, oh my,
a poorly crafted poem, maybe mediocre, beloved by
unsophisticated backward simple folk, just too
ignorant to know better like the learned elite do.
But when I was a child it had been set to music, and
Walt Disney's animators created a lyrical cartoon to brand
a generation's tuneful imagination to never forget
these words, this poem, this song, this sight, this duet
of a poet's rapture at a common object of great beauty
that so lifted my heart so tearfully
as I remember the trees I have planted over decades
that grew and bloomed and died in sunshine and shade
cut down by borer, blight, high winds, power saws, decay
disease, and drought. No photograph can ever again display
the intricate design, subtle colors, elegant details, the majesty
I think that I shall never see

A poem lovely as a tree.
and for Joyce, poem was a two-syllable word.
Now when pronounced only a pregnant one is heard.
However, when it comes to a lovely tree,
a flowering dogwood, *cornus florida,* is the one for me.
Saucer magnolias, flowering crabapples, cherries, pears,
can also inspire colored pencils, paper, and a folding chair.
It was a good thing too, because a fungus disease
has killed or damaged the dogwood trees.
A few years back I returned to a city park
in Richmond, Virginia where I once viewed remark-
ably large dogwood trees all around me

as I sat with oil paints and studiously
recorded every color nuance and detail
of dogwood blossoms on a wooden panel
in such delight, only to see they were all gone.
Only the huge sweet bay magnolias from that long
ago springtime paradise were there with evergreens
and empty spaces where the dogwoods had once been.
It was unkempt, seemingly uncared for and a place
I was then told of muggings, sexual assaults, disgrace-
ful violent acts at night, and even daylight. The trees?
The missing dogwoods were wiped out by disease,
the dogwood anthracnose that had blighted
woodlands and gardens and lawns sited
with those beauties. But beyond blossoms,
even leaves of so many trees like maples, oaks, sweet gums,
elms, aspens, catalpas, horse chestnuts, on and on,
such delights to hold, behold in every season
especially the brilliant yellows, golds, oranges, scarlets, wine-reds
of autumn, and they were all found on the five-pointed
star-shaped leaves of my sweet gum surrounded by softer hues
and mottled greens of every shade and color even the purples, blues
of plums and spruces. The visual enchantment of tree shapes, forms
bilateral or freely flowing, towering and shading to cool and warm
and shield from wind and storm, and also sculpted bonsai are like poems?
These words of black on white that strive to become
founts of images and sights that have filled a reader's mind
to be mined, called forth from vaults of sensory events aligned
with the words., even crafted with skill and symmetry, can never be
A poem lovely as a tree.

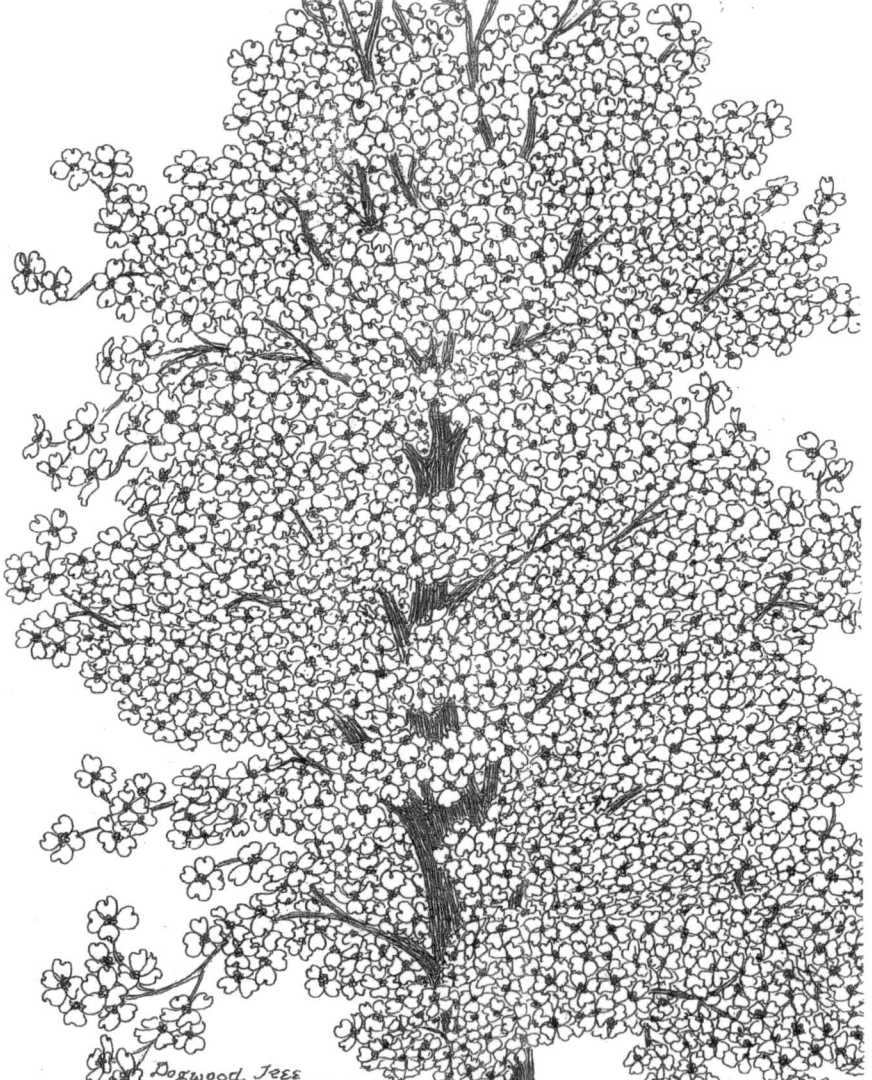

A tree whose hungry mouth is prest
Now we open the major metaphorical stage chest.
The tree is dressed in human or critter costume,
as if now the poet wants to groom or be a groom
to embrace visually and imaginatively surround
this loved object to see roots reaching in the ground
to be like tongues and teeth to push and suck
the nutrients in the soil, to feed and shuck
from the muck, to hold, support with a broad base
the trunk and branches. But where's the face?
The metaphor becomes odd because like a frown,
the body of a human drops vertically down
below the mouth, whereas the body of a tree
rises vertically up above the ground, but there be
many critters like sheep, rabbits, and robins that also ingest
like *A tree whose hungry mouth is prest*

Against the earth's sweet flowing breast;
Ah, the earth mother with the tree as babe whether sprout
or giant sequoia and every other tree out and about
at the breast of Mother Earth. Add some fertilizer or manure and mulch
to counteract the Roundup and Weed B Gon and other such
poisonous chemicals that now in food and water inhibit growth
and steadily kill. Don't forget to water during drought.
That's how I lost the magnolia and a red maple lost its color.
However, the local nursery has a compound for when that does occur,
and I need to go get more and apply it around the tree again.
This spring and summer we've been blessed with rain
and the nipple's dripping for those roots that spread compressed
Against the earth's sweet flowing breast;

A tree that looks at God all day,
Where are those eyes that are looking up?
Far above the mouth sucking the ground close up,
sort of at the top, or maybe the total tree is eyes,

since God exists and could be seen not just at sunrise,
but everywhere, even underground in the well-endowed
Mother Nature, and not just in the clouds.
The tree is focused on the spiritual orbit,
the source of abundant life, indeed, embodies it,
and inspires us to stop and gaze and reluctant turn away
from *a tree that looks at God all day*

And lifts her leafy arms to pray;
Ah, the tree is female, a daughter one might say
of Mother Nature. The arms are presumably branches,
but limbs would include legs lifting up from the mouth that latches
onto the earth below. The trunk presumably is the spine
as the human anatomical metaphor walks its fault line.
Again the tree is focused on the spiritual from which it grows
and murmurs through the leaves as the breeze blows
the sound the tree sings night and day
and lefts her leafy arms to pray;

A tree that may in Summer wear
What is the clothing of a tree? It's bark when it is bare,
so it must be the leaves. With few exceptions, it is green
in summer. That color with the evergreens is the scene
outdoors. Since there *will* be green, what *may* be there?
A tree that may in Summer wear

A nest of robins in her hair;
The vision here is a weeping willow because there
will be skinny leaves and branches falling down
from a horizontal circular crown,
which could support a bird nest like an ornamental rose
or comb on human hair. But if leaves are the clothes,
how are they also the hair? Ah, the chameleon metaphor!

Some varieties of trees have the sexes separated for
the masculine and feminine parts, but most do not
and are hermaphrodites. Joyce Kilmer is besot
and wants to love his tree like a woman, so there's
A nest of robins in her hair.

Upon whose bosom snow has lain;
Jack Frost is taking liberties during dormancy, and none complain,
but where is the bosom? Snow can cover, even blanket
branches, and evergreens have lumpy clumps that make it,
if a small couple hump together, look like breasts.
The branches are the bosom., and the hand of Jack Frost never rests
until the thaw. Let Winter throw the tree his lacy counterpane
Upon whose bosom snow has lain;

Who intimately lives with rain.
She cannot live without the rains, so he reigns.
She also needs the sun, but she can make do with the shade.
While some trees get by on little, no tree that's made
can survive without water. That's what drought's all about.
So a few years back, while hauling gallons in a cart
to water the trees after weeks without a drop, I thought
that was what was ailing my big beautiful shady green ash tree.
So preoccupied with water, I did not see
or recognize some early stages of the attack
of the green ash borers. If I could just go back
with what I know now of when and how to save
that ash tree from the borer epidemic using what they've
in the tree nursery trade come up with for early intervention.
The next year was too late for the insecticide injection
to stop the fate of certain death. I watched it fight valiantly and cried
as slowly, slowly each leaf and twig and branch and tree limb died.
Borers attacked the green ashes first, so I was able to pay
the nurserymen to inject two white ash trees and slay
the worms tunneling within their bark.

They are still alive and thrive as a landmark
of how I could have stopped the borer had I but known
in time. I thought too that lack of water caused ingrown
canker die back in my apple tree, but I was told
by the Davey Tree expert that it was fire blight and nothing sold
could stop it. The grounds crew cut it down to keep
the blight from spreading, but were too cheap
or underpaid to cut down the ash trees and left mine,
a huge skeleton of winter's black etching lines
to dominate my view out my patio window
for two years despite my paying a nursery for two trees to grow
to replace it and the blighted apple tree planted nearby.
I did save after the drought a small red oak that would die
unless cut back to the lowest branches which I did,
and it came back and is growing well. God forbid
it be vandalized like another tree I paid to be planted
with the permission of the board of directors that granted
and marked the place, but some boys tore off all the bark,
and I watched those new leaves turn their red autumn color then dark
and drop forever never to come back. That aforementioned drought
did weaken my 40 year-old sweet gum tree as it was sited almost out
of its normal range so that it would take longer than other trees nearby
to sprout its leaves in spring. These last few years the sky
has rained buckets and all trees are expanding fulsomely
as did the sweet gum until a storm split it in half tragically
revealing its rotted core. But it quickly was cut down
and the living roots beneath the flattened trunk shaped like a crown
sent up new stalks with those lovely five-pointed star-shaped leaves
I loved so well. I was able to get permission to weave
a wire fence around a clump of such shoots protecting them
from the grounds crew and their weed whackers as they trim
around the stump, but a harsh winter and May freeze
killed the shoots, and also many emerging flowers and leaves.

It starved the awakening roots and branches
of many young trees. The warm rains that followed and the sun sustain
Who intimately lives with rain.

Poems are made by fools like me.
In many ways a poem is like a tree.
The title or a line could be the seed
that the imagination fertilizes so it can breed
all kinds of images from nouns and verbs and prepositions,
remembered rhymes, metaphors and alliterations.
The lines can grow to stanzas or like bonsai be small and few,
a tiny crafted masterpiece, or like Ginsberg's "Howl!", a monster stew.
But now I'm mixing metaphors just to get a rhyme,
so I'll return to trees and a wide length of lines this time
like a trunk with jagged bark on both sides if the lines are centered.
However, looks are not the major thing. What matters is if it's remembered.
A poem needs a reader like a tree needs rain.
It cannot live without it, and not just one drop, but a water main
of readers gushing like a thunderstorm that may go but return again
to take root in many minds that fertilize it then
share it, put it to music, and picture it in art,
memorize it, quote it, transplant it to the heart.
All this happened to Kilmer's "Trees" almost a century ago.
Then it experienced a drought, and poems other poets sow
crowded it to just a stem, a line old people mumble absently,
Poems are made by fools like me.

But only God can make a tree.
How does God make a tree? Well, we
know something of His methods because we have participated
many times in the making. I live in a development created
out of a bur oak hickory woodland, and the builder
decided to keep a lot of the old trees placing near
and around them the townhouses and streets.

However, the buildings and their upkeep beats
that of the trees, and dooms them to a slow decay.
Because of the tap root, bur oaks don't transplant, so they
had planted evergreens, silver maples, green and white ash,
Washington hawthorns, elms, ornamentals, and even asked
residents and homeowners who lived on the edge
of the woods to plant their own choices. This privilege
was revoked as years passed to getting permission from
the board of directors. I have planted over forty years some
forty trees with and without my husband. Of that number
twenty-five are still alive, but more depressing, under
one third of the old bur oaks still survive. Stewardship
has been lacking and children and adults tear and whip
the limbs and leaves and even destroy whole trees.
God gives and takes away despite my prayers and pleas.
Is this all God's doing? Out in front between my house
and the house next door was a pile of stones, a coarse
way to kill a bur oak stump, but adding top soil and manure
I turned it to a flower garden of crocus and annuals to insure
it was not an eyesore. Acorns that squirrels buried there would sprout,
and I or the landscaping crew would pull or dig them out.
As I aged the yearly work of the garden became too hard,
so around a decade ago I asked permission of the board
to let one of those bur oak sprouts be allowed to grow.
I spread manure and mulch around but a bur oak is slow
and takes its time because it's programmed to live a long,
long time. How long? I counted the rings of one that looked so sturdy,
strong
but died recently. I made a drawing before it was cut down
guessing it was three hundred based upon its size and other stumps
around,
and sure enough, this tree had sprouted from an acorn even before
settlers came this far west and the Revolutionary War.

Over 300 year old
dead bur oak tree
Beverley Ross Enright

My baby bur oak is now as tall as where the roof begins above
the second story. The God that made this tree used my desire and love
along with the acorn, squirrel, rain, sunshine, air's molecules
and the wire fence surrounding the stem then trunk, and rules
restraining the landscaping crew. To say I made it is untrue,
and each tree that we, I planted was already planted and sold through
a nursery or Arbor Day. All those trees that grew and still survive
and also the ones that died, involved a slew of other people to be alive.
So this is God. The God that gives and nurtures, protects and cares for trees
is also the God of the borer, fire blight, human ignorance, and disease.
All our days are numbered, even ancient old oak trees, and the causes
of death and destruction, murder and extinction, garbage and plastic straws,
whether natural disasters, or human-made disasters, are akin
for human nature is of Nature and all life is covered with some skin like sin.
"It rains upon the just and the unjust." While all plants and animals need
water, too much rain can flood cities, drown and destroy, speed
into a hurricane or tsunami. Did God make climate change?
The same way He makes or kills a tree? Does it seem so strange
that Boxer, the good horse, that continues to work harder until
all his strength is gone and finds he's sent to the slaughter house at the will
of lying leaders who have the power to determine another's fate,
even the fate of planet Earth. But if you have not read *Animal Farm* and can't relate,
I will now remind you of the story of Jesus's agonizing prayers in Gethsemane,
the trial and crucifixion. Did God really make that happen? And will it always be

the poisonous ingredients, the powerful few that will undo what good people can accomplish with love, nurture, hard work, sacrifice, and who would
make the earth sustain healthy life to end always in tragedy?
That tree that sprouted from a bur oak acorn a squirrel had let be that I had asked the crew to spare a decade ago now comforts me.
But only God can make a tree.

FEBRUARY SPRING

It won't last of course.
These days without even a jacket on
fooling some flowers and trees
that will freeze
and the birds that come back
will fly south again
and the animals that leave hibernation
will go back to their caves
and holes in the ground
as we too will huddle in our houses.
Jack Frost will come back
to bite our noses
and bundle us up
in packages with foam peanuts
and air pockets.
But for now
in this unreal warmth
we stroll beside the skeletal trees
and brown lawns
and dead foliage
like finding a gingerbread house
in a clearing while lost in a dark woods
whose cookie door opens
to a freeze locker
and the beckoning President's Day sales
come with the icy prick
of fine print.
But that is next week
as we ride this warm furry brown
donkey through the streets
and jubilant crowds
shout "Hosanna!"

--Beverley Rose Enright

"LESS IS MORE"

Don't tell that to a starving man
or a thirsty woman or child.
Don't tell that to a hard-working farmer
whose crops die during a drought.
Don't tell that to the homeless
freezing without coats in the cold.
Don't tell that to a blind or deaf person
or someone without arms or legs,
a stomach, a bowel, or a functioning kidney.
Don't tell that to the old.
Don't tell that to the woman whose child
did not survive the car crash,
the kidnapper, the bullet, or the flood.
Don't say that when the house burns down,
the job's gone, the life savings are stolen.
Less can be loss.

Don't tell that to the teacher or boss,
or on checks when paying the bills.
Don't say that when the business goes bankrupt,
or when cleaning or doing your chores.
Don't say that to the doctor
about doing your exercises,
or to the dentist about cleaning your teeth.
Don't write that to the IRS about not filing your form,
and don't say that about spending time with the kids.
Don't tell that to your spouse, your family, or friends,
about hugs and kisses, and fond compliments.
Don't say that about saying "I love you."
Less can be not enough.

Even in a song or a poem what's unwritten
may well be what needs to be said,
and the passion that's checked,
and the time that's not given
will be useless after you're dead.

A CHRISTMAS CAROL, 2018

> *"You were always such a good man of business, Jacob"*
> *"Mankind was my business"*
> Charles Dickens, *A Christmas Carol*

Ralph Nader, whose candidacy for US president
defeated Al Gore, the VP who schooled himself
about the climate global crisis when something
could have been done, is the same
Ralph Nader who wrote about the conflict
between private enterprise and the common good.
The Great Pacific Garbage Patch is bigger
than twice the size of Texas.
It is bigger than the other four garbage patches
floating in the gyres of the oceans and seas.
It is full of plastic and nine feet deep.
Tons of plastic are found in the guts of dead beached whales
and pounds in the guts of dead sea turtles washed ashore.
It is now in the guts of wildlife and people,
and can eventually make all life sterile.
Humans don't need nuclear bombs to destroy all life.
Plastic will do the job.
Planet Earth has now become Tiny Tim.
Will the legions of Ebenezer Scrooges
repent and save it?
The winter light is dim.

HOW TO MAKE A GREAT TOSSED SALAD

All you need is a soft prolonged kiss
on the back of a large leaf of lettuce
and each hand cupped around
a tomato with the thumbs
rubbing and pressing the stem ends,
and there is no need
for the oil or dressing
or even the small slender cucumber.

THE HOT SEXPOT

She had a name and was a child of God, of course,
and a mind and spirit inside her voluptuous body.
Her mother had raised her to be a fine pianist,
but was defeated by her glamorous face.

She shared small attic rooms with me
and another young woman down on our luck
and on our own away from home and family
in a boarding house back in the boomer sixties.

She would sometimes sit cross-legged with a record,
a vinyl playing Ravel's "Bolero" while a burning wick
wafted incense as she smoked her forbidden joint,
seeking another world more like the one described

in her favorite novel, Heinlein's *Stranger
in a Strange Land*. I've never read it all,
it did not grab me, but she quoted from it
in place of the Bible she had long discarded.

Her life had lost direction, and she dragged me
to the college bars one night protecting her
from being picked up as she flirted flagrantly
while I, ignored and shy, watched and worried.

I think we both got back to our rooms intact,
but I, who seldom drank any alcohol, had drunk
three brandy alexanders, while she had downed
many rum cokes and vodka somethings I forget.

An intellectual gay man I knew I found one day
sitting in the landing waiting and found to my dismay
and disappointment not for me but her.
I asked her later what she thought of him I once admired.

She shrugged a noncommittal "eh" and went back
to boasting how she had made a fur-lined jock strap
for her clinical psychologist. I don't think she still
was attending therapy sessions with him then.

She lost her job, ran out of cash, and had to leave
even those cheap rooms that rented for ten bucks,
and the Mom she had abandoned came and got her,
and I have never heard what happened to her since.

LINES AFTER READING RANDALL MANN'S POEM "ORDER"

What a seductive symmetry!
It speaks to me like geometry,
ovals, isosceles triangles,
hyperbolas, diamonds, hexagons.

It looks to me like my body,
the mirror image of arms and legs,
hands, feet, fingers, toes,
buttocks, breasts, my nose,

going there and back again
in morning and evening commutes.
Antique Western hang-up, Asians scoff.
Quilt makers love it.

Apples, pears, pecans, and walnuts,
the silhouettes of spruce and fir,
going up and coming down
stairs, ladders, and elevators,

a bounce, reflections in the water,
the brain's bilateral design
still has a difference in the details,
in right and left, a subtle shift.

In left and right a subtle shift
still has a difference in the details,
the brain's bilateral design,
a bounce, reflections in the water,

ladders, stairs, and elevators
going up and coming down,
the silhouettes of spruce and fir,
apples, pears, pecans, and walnuts.

Quilt makers love it.
Antique Western hang-up, Asians scoff
in morning and evening commutes
going there and back again.

Buttocks, breasts, my nose,
feet, hands, fingers, toes,
the mirror image of arms and legs,
it looks to me like my body.

Diamonds, hyperbolas, hexagons,
ovals, isosceles triangles,
it speaks to me like geometry.
What a seductive symmetry!

WHAT GOES AROUND

to Weldon Kees

Willie Pickins jazzes "Jesus Loves Me"
on his piano. A five-year-old is shot
by street gang crossfire in Chicago.
Angelina Jolie has had her breasts removed.
Bosch's "The Temptation of St. Anthony"
hangs slightly slanted. My dove's white empty cage
is clean. The war in Syria fills the T-V screen.
Pickins jazzes "Jesus Loves Me".

Bosch's "Temptation of St. Anthony" has bawdy
imps cavorting in the lower left hand corner.
Angelina Jolie has had her breasts removed.
A five-year-old is shot walking home from school
by street gangs. Mr. Dovebar's empty cage is white
and clean. He flew up from my hand high in a tree.
I scream as I slice my finger cutting onions.
The war in Syria fills the T-V screen.

Street gang warfare in Chicago kills
a five-year-old. Bosch's "Temptation of St. Anthony"
has bawdy imps. Mr. Dovebar did not fly back to me.
I scream as I slice my finger cutting onions.
Angelina Jolie has had her breasts removed.
The T-V screen is full of war. The empty cage
in the corner by the white piano is clean.
Willie Pickins jazzes "Jesus Loves Me".

A FUGING TUNE

The praise team rocks "My Hope Is Built".
Another rosary comes in the mail.
My pet rabbits are digging holes inside
the backyard fence. Tiny black bugs
slowly eat my wall-to-wall carpeting.
My fungal toenails look like ginger root.
Only a dozen people have been born
down in Antarctica. The praise Team rocks.

Only a dozen people have been born in Antarctica.
Pope Francis tells the Catholics they should not breed
like rabbits. My wall-to-wall is losing pile
that hides black specks of bugs. Fungal toenails
look like ginger root. "My Hope Is Built"
on a rock defense. Three rosaries
are holed up in my purse. The praise team comes
on a packaged CD in the mail.

My rabbits are digging holes escaping
from under the backyard fence. Only a dozen
people have been born in Antarctica.
Black specks of bugs pepper my wall-to-wall
shaving it. What roots toenail fungus out?
Lamisil corrodes the liver. Another rosary
comes in the mail from Franciscans, and
the praise team rocks "My Hope Is Built".

COUNTER VIEWPOINTS

No more MacDonald's hamburgers for me.
One hundred thousand people say that they
would move to Mars. No butterflies have visited
my garden. Mount Everest is higher
than the tallest skyscrapers. The green ash borer
has killed my handsome green ash tree. My finger nails
tear off as if by a paper shredder. My arteries are clogged.
Methane beef cattle pass is a greenhouse gas.

One hundred thousand people say that they
would move to Mars. Mount Everest
dwarfs the highest towers. Some insects
are beautiful like butterflies, but not
the green ash borer. My garden vegetables
are better than big Macs to help my stents
keep my arteries unclogged. Methane gas
tears the air and shreds the atmosphere.

Borers have shredded and clogged the arteries
of my magnificent green ash tree. The atmosphere
on Mars is thinner and colder than atop Mount Everest.
MacDonald's burgers come from beef cattle moving
in hundreds of thousand herds all farting methane.
Too many people are killing our planet. Paper
butterflies float down from high skyscraper windows,
and no more tears for me in greenhouse gardens.

A MAN WHO CAN USE HIS HANDS

Any man who can use his hands
Is always needed and desired.
Undervalued, he's really grand;
He fixes the broken and unwired.

Any man who can use his hands
To sort and pound and screw and suction,
To strip and saw and paint and sand,
To take apart what does not function,

And put it together so it's right,
Who sees the problem and understands
With his focused brain and foresight
Connected to his skillful hands

That shape and stroke and pull and press,
That fits the tools to insure the thing's
Constructed strong, and clears the mess
So all works well, has angel's wings.

More important than the man who rules
Or the man who dreams or makes the plans
Is the man who makes the machines and tools,
Is the man who can use his hands.

GLOSA ON A POEM BY ALEX GILDZEN AS A MEISTERLIEDE

>*in memory of Patrick Enright,
>who loved Wagner's operas*

*Das waren hochbedürft'ge Meister
von Lebensmüh bedrängte Geister
in ihrer Nöten Wildnis
sie schufen sich ein Bildnis
dass ihnen bliebe
der Jugendiebe
ein Angedenken, klar und fest
dran sich der Lenzerkennen lasst*
>--Richard Wagner, DIE MEISTERSINGER VON NÜRNBERG

*Those moments are risks
we dare not paint on rocks*

*for others to misunderstand
but having stood*

*we sing the moments
from our minds*

*and dance the rose
till dawn's rise.*
>--untitled poem by Alex Gildzen

Erster Bar

Those moments are risks
on a warm late Spring-like afternoon

when petunias, marigolds, ageratum croon,
I met and walked with a handsome fellow
through rainbows of pink and blue and yellow.
Those moments are risks

we dare not paint on rocks
His face was a fount of song and tune,
of crackerjack, lollipop, and macaroon
and the painted stones by the pussy willow
sent me back to my room with a stone like a swallow.
we dare not paint on rocks

Abgesang

for others to misunderstand
I painted a Byzantine angel's face
and gave it to him as an artist's embrace
for others to misunderstand

but having stood
so we would not touch, not then, or now,
but simply be, like a horse or a cow.
but having stood

Zweiter Bar

we sing the moments
and so we parted, and so we stay
to write and draw and paint and pray,
and in every song and picture and poem
that directs our steps toward that emerald home
we sing the moments

from our minds
into our hearts, the memory of that day

with the colors of youth and springtime's display
to warm our old hearts when we're alone
and the time for romance has long since flown
from our minds

Dritter Bar

and dance the rose
I wore a dress then with deep golden roses
splashed like a garden from sprinklers and hoses
on soft cotton satin for a mime of a dance
with a prince for a whisper, a whiff of romance
and dance the rose

till dawn's rise.
He gave me this poem and quickly it closes,
"a lily of a day", or what a night's dream encloses,
and every thrust of our long life's lance
has battled and risked by design or circumstance
till dawn's rise.

OUR MARRIAGE IS A MUNDANE MIRACLE

I shall sleep with you tonight
Though I've longed to be in others' arms,
Was moved far stronger by their charms,
Dazzled by their greater light,
But I shall sleep with you tonight.

I shall eat with you today
Though I've preferred words that others say,
And their speaking style and deeper voice,
And their sorrow and rejoice,
But I shall eat with you today.

I shall walk with you today
Though other legs have had more grace,
Though other feet a brighter step,
And though they go a sweeter way,
Yet I shall walk with you today.

For in each bit of less than best,
Of worst than most that I embrace,
I know I see that blood stained face,
And am received as I receive
You each day until my final rest.

YOU NEVER REALLY ARE DIVORCED

There's no more sexual intercourse,
and you seldom speak to each other, still,
you never really are divorced.

Your marriage wandered off its course
to Antarctica and an oil spill,
and no more sexual intercourse.

But though you both jumped off the horse,
and called it quits, bye-bye, splitsville,
you never really are divorced.

Despite the pangs of regret, remorse,
fault-finding, blame, guilt-trips, ill-will,
and no more sexual intercourse,

eventually you'll see the source
of what united you until
you felt you had to get divorced.

You're still connected by the force
of memories of what worked well
with love and sexual intercourse,
so you never really are divorced.

UNDEFINED

Division by zero is undefined.
This is true mathematically
for every number to infinity
including zero.
Many tricks
with algebraic manipulations
have been devised
to keep zero out
of the denominator.
But not in all cases,
like ours, for example.
Consider the numbers one and zero,
the binary bedrock
for the amazing abundance
of technological miracles
that have the potential to connect
all human beings on earth
via a web of computer chips,
are also the erotic symbols
for the two sexes.
Division by one is possible
although it changes nothing.
One divided by one is one,
and zero divided by one is zero.
But one or zero divided by zero
is undefined.
Therefore if nothing divides us,
what are we then?
Not friends, not lovers, not spouses,
but what? Not nothing, but something
that's undefined.

INTIMATIONS OF DIVINITY

Shifting her eyes
From the sparkling snow
She gazed up to see
A nimbus glow.

ICON OF CHRIST IN GLORY

This vision was told by Ezekiel,
and again by Saint John the Divine.
Four creatures with wings fill the corners;
holding the gospels, they shine.

This vision shows rainbows encircling,
translucently colored like jewels,
on clouds soft as lambs wool in springtime
that billow like ripples in pools.

This vision has choirs of angels,
and elders with lamp stands aflame,
and six-winged seraphim, singing,
all praising the Almighty's Name.

This vision of gold radiating
around the white garments of light
shows God, Spirit, Christ, One in union
enthroned in majesty's might.

THE HOLY FACE

A miraculous imprint of Christ
was etched on a square of white linen
that was pressed when held to His face.
This legend is not in the gospels
and is told in a few different ways.
One is that Christ appeared to a prince
sick unto death who entreated of Jesus
to heal his body and then asked for a sign,
a proof of Christ's presence on cloth.
Another tells of a woman on the way
Jesus walked and carried the cross up the mount.
She pressed her cloth to His face
to wipe off the blood and the sweat,
but the print showed no blood or the marks
of the brutal scourging or thorns
that circled his brow, all erased,
as if it revealed the foretold risen face.
Other names for this icon exist:
"Veronica", "Mandylion", "The Face of Christ
Not Created by Human Hand."
But an artist's hand painted the icon,
often on linen that was glued to the wood.
The artist had fasted and prayed
that the Spirit of God would take over his hand
as he painted Christ's Holy Face.

TO TED

Another singer has gone to glory
And yet I still abide,
My spirit stuck in this aging body,
My link to heaven inside.

I shout my joy for the ageless story
With those I stand beside;
Together we sing the shape note stanzas
Of music magnified.

A music I'll hear and sing forever
After my flesh has died.
And join the spirits of those departed
With Christ forever tied.

THE "USELESS" FLOWERS

Give me the flowers while I live,
Something to cheer me on.
Useless the flowers you may give
After the soul is gone.
    "Odem", p. 340, 1991 Sacred Harp Songbook

The flowers in funeral parlors
Are not there for the dead.
Their scent and beauty soothe sorrow.
They bless the bereaved instead.

I buy my bouquets and plant flowers
To cheer me while I live.
Of course I am grateful to get them
If you are inspired to give.

To fuss and whine about funerals
and all the flowers put there
to comfort the friends and family
is more than this heart can bear.

TO JUDY

The motions of the mind may tangle,
The movements of the body cramp,
The bones may break, blood vessels clog,
Yet keep a sacred stamp.

It's hard to watch loved ones decay
And crumble down who stood.
It's sad to hear the voices fray
But memories are good.

The journey of a life goes up
And down and out and in,
And how it ends is not the sum;
What counts is where it's been.

IN A MINOR TURNING TO MAJOR KEY

> *the trouble with poetry is*
> *that it encourages the writing of more poetry.*
>   Billy Collins, *"The Trouble with Poetry"*

I drink wine sometimes,
but prefer grape juice
which is healthier,
and I suppose the grapes more so,
especially for minors.

My husband, a curmudgeon,
preferred the minor key,
but all hymns whether
major or minor
are beloved by me.

Well, maybe not all hymns,
but the key was not
the key signature,
but rather the tune
or verse.

If God is trampling
out the vintage
where the grapes of wrath
are composted,
where's the glory?

One person's great poem
is another's sour grape,
be the poet major
or minor, or not much
of a poet like me.

Hallelujah!

TO PHILIP DACEY DYING OF LEUKEMIA

I know you from your poetry and email.
I never met your body, I met your soul.
Your body will go to fire and a deep hole
after a dissection that will unveil

what parts can be recycled, what part can heal
by replacement another's body to make it whole.
I know you from your poetry and email.
I never met your body, I met your soul.

Your soul will jet to heaven like airmail
yet stay in poems witty, condensed, and droll
like your messages to me heal and console,
I love you for your poetry and email.

Face   Benedez Rose Enright

PHILIP DACEY MEETS WALT WHITMAN, GERARD MANLEY HOPKINS, AND THOMAS EAKINS IN HEAVEN

I.

What do you think has become of the young and old men?
And what do you think has become of the women and children?
They are alive and well somewhere.
. . .
And to die is different from what anyone supposed and luckier.
                                    Walt Whitman, *"Song of Myself"*

Walt Whitman in his glorified body like the photograph that prefaces
his *Leaves of Grass,* and the Thomas Eakins portrait, but both
translated to an inner radiance bursting forth like grass
and his uncut hair, the body electric charged eternal
robust yet courtly is an introduction to the poet's guild
gliding along on a river of song.
He greets Philip Dacey with the all-so-familiar lines
echoing from his aura like the memorized refrains
voiced in a chorus from the deep wine cellars
of countless celestial brains.

II.

In a flash, at a trumpet crash,
I am all at once what Christ is, since he is what I am, and
This Jack, joke, poor potsherd, patch, matchwood, immortal diamond,
Is immortal diamond.

                      Gerard Manley Hopkins, *"That Nature is a Heraclitean Fire and of the comfort of the Resurrection"*

Gerard Manley Hopkins greets Philip Dacey with the words "Since imitation is the sincerest compliment, I thank you for the book of poems you wrote as though you were me." And he comes beaming in a whitened priest's habit glowing with heavenly glory, but still gently advises Phil that the ending poem that supposes to take place in heaven imagines such things of earthly pleasures unneeded in heaven as they are fouled with pain and humiliations absent where love abounds purely with dazzling colors and celestial organ music and angelic choruses full of bird calls, whispering breezes, bubbling waterfalls, and deep ocean murmurs of OM.

III.

I have seen big painting here. When I had looked at all the paintings by all the masters I had known I could not help saying to myself all the time, it's very pretty, but it is not all yet.
                    Thomas Eakins in a letter to Benjamin Eakins.

Thomas Eakins appears in his now youthful nude body transformed and luminous beyond nature and greets Phil saying, "I thank you, Phil, for the book of poetry you wrote to honor me. It is an honest book, a big picture artfully detailed and uses words as I used my brush as it probes my life and work and what it meant to the others who viewed it and participated in it. Now come and view the glories of this new life! The artistry! The intensity! Such love surrounds me! Such love!"

SWAN COTTAGE

For Philip Koplow

Gone is the cottage
And you are gone too.
Gone like the swan
That once danced with you.

That dance in the photo
At the funeral display
Gave us a view
Of you both at play.

And the swan gave his name
To your home in Augusta
Though the swan ceased to come
To the lake near your porch.

You with your wife filled
The cottage with swans
On paper and pottery,
On stained glass and pillows.

A place filled with summer
And sunlight and breezes.
A place to repose and compose
A music to wind chimes,

Like the nectar that filled
The feeder for hummingbirds,
Like the crash of the thunder
Trumpeting rain.

The ferry that crosses
The Ohio River
Is the ferry that takes you
From this bank to the other.

The cottage now floats
By the banks of our memories
Like the swan is gone
Flown into the past.

THE GOLDEN SWAN

A white swan glides across the lake
shining in the dazzling sun drops
as the sun descends in a late afternoon
like a white boat heaped with gold
doubloons, caskets, and snake-necked urns.

This golden avatar of yellow sunbeams
caressing the shadows that peek beneath the waves
as I gaze intently instantly takes flight
straight toward that blinding source of light
dissolving into pixels, blurring to my sight,
to vanish in a sun of yellow roses.

EARTHWORM

My lacy castings lay
        like copper coins
to give my lair away
        where tunnel joins
the air for robins prey
        and pull my loins
        in easy slide
on this earth's muddy clay
        amusement ride.

ENDANGERED

The monarch butterflies are now endangered
because of climate change biologists say.
In my youth there were so many every summer
that I could see them in the backyard every day.

So much of what was common is almost gone.
I went online to get a list of endangered birds,
and when I chose to print it out, the pages
flowed such a pile of paper I stopped the words

so as to keep some ink remaining in my cartridge.
So much for choosing among those birds to write poems.
And there are also the mammals, fish, amphibians,
Reptiles and insects if you care at all about them.

Most people don't or they would not be endangered.
So much such life that used to be so common
and as populous as the people, now in growing numbers,
once killed flocks of pigeons that blocked the sun,

and kill each other in wars, murders, and mass shootings,
poisoning air, earth, water, causing cancer and starvation,
though technologically all could be fed and all of life
sustained. History tells us over population

suffers a natural correction like the lemmings
who jump off cliffs to bring their numbers down
within the limits of resources for their kind.
So many women now go childless and teens drown

their fears of the future in suicide addictions.
The greed of homo sapiens sapiens for destruction
in all its guises would take the whole of life
on this planet away with their self extinction.

All this despite the knowledge and intelligence
and the gifts that species has evolved with;
the faith and vision and wisdom of the few
are sabotaged by the many whose growing birth

of ignorance, stupidity, and indifference has cursed
all that might and could have been prevented
had those that knew and saw and cared been listened to
by people with power who make all life endangered.

Endangered Earth and Lifeless Siblings
Beverley Rose Enright

FRAGMENT OF SOLITUDE

I am like a tree-of-heaven
planted behind the dunes
trying to hold back the oceans
rising as the ice sheets melt
and the carbon dioxide
turns the seas toxic
as it burns all the land
and turns it to desert.

TO A BUTTERFLY

O little lonely lovely butterfly,
You bless my presence with your spark of joy
Reminding me how frail is life and love.

So very fragile like a clear blue sky
Can change and darken, smoke as bombs destroy
Reminding how hard hate is to remove.

O sad is earth endowed for every eye
With abundant awesome scenes all could enjoy
Now threatened with a death none can remove.

For every person now who sees you fly
Are many who only know you as a toy,
pictures, jewels, quilts, opera, a glove,

Embroidered, painted, paper folded, dry.
The many ways your image now employed
Exists in greater numbers than now move

In nature's world alongside fireflies,
Mosquitoes, moths, wasps, gnats and dragonflies,
Cicadas, locusts, spiders, bees evolved

With worms, ants, roaches, bedbugs, lice,
Ticks, termites, insect friends and destroyers
That crawl and hide below and fly above.

Most precious and revered of those that fly,
You are because from caterpillar coy
You hide inside cocooned as in a cave

That opens, O surprise! My butterfly!
From darkness into light, despair to joy,
And from a world of death to one of love.

GLOBAL WARNING

A certain tree needs a fungus near to grow.
    Smart bees cross-pollinate.
Dumb bees stay in one tree to blow the show
    and make the fruit third-rate.
Earth is more needful than people know.

The strangler fig and Spanish moss drape hosts
    long after they have died,
and kudzu carpets woods to shape green ghosts
    of the dying trees inside.
Nature's revenge on man's mistaken boasts
    is a man-poisoned tide.
If we don't become fit husband to earth-wife,
we'll make the earth unfit for any life.

ASK THE BUTTERFLIES

All children hear about
how caterpillars spin
inside cocoons, come out
as butterflies.

And children learn of Jesus
who died, was put inside
a tomb that opened for us,
his life revived.

The Monarch butterflies
now face extinction's fate
because the corporate lies
make greed inflate.

Profits mean more than lives
of people, plants,; those words
and deeds doom fish, beehives.
flowers, birds.

They make poisons to sell
to kill unwanted weeds
and insects but don't tell
all those it feeds.

They poison water, earth,
destroy, drill and spill
oil, plastic, waste for wealth,
take health and kill.

All like Monsanto liars
in power who truth resist,
all climate change deniers,
hear scientists.

Ask the butterflies
as now they fly away
before the last one dies
and hear them say:

"We are passing away,
you are passing away,
all are passing away,
to Judgment Day."

SELECTIONS FROM SONNET SEQUENCES:

SONNETS TO THE PSALMS

100 SONNETS TO THE CALCULUS

from SONNETS TO THE PSALMS

SONNETS 1

> *Like a tree planted by the rivers of water*
> *Psalm 1:3a KJV*

So many do not understand
how desperately we need the trees.
They burn them down to clear the land
nor heed the warnings of a few degrees

hotter yearly temperatures or pleas
to save the habitat of birds and fish
that vanish to extinction when trees vanish.
Aren't trees but our front lines against the desert?

Trees make the oxygen we breathe to live.
Trees shield from wind and rain and blazing skies.
Trees hold the moisture that would vaporize
away and dry the soil that would erode and give

the land to gullies and advancing dunes.
Without the trees, the earth's a barren moon.

I do not like you, Mr. T.
Your new wealth bought a forested estate,
but you would not keep a single tree.
You shocked your neighbors to an angry hate.

They tried to get the law to stop your saws.
Those trees had stood for centuries; now fate
for money put their lives within your claws.
Why does the great Sahara increase in Africa?

For trees don't grow on money but on years;
ring after ring their trunks record the rounds
they've used in reaching upward. How it spears
my heart to see you speedily cut them down!

Time will remember this when you are old.
Your treeless house and land remains unsold.

I do not like you, nation of Brazil.
Your tropical rainforests grow
on unexpectedly unfertile soil
where shallow-rooted soaring palms and ferns

are wrapped by thick lianas and orchid vines
and make an Eden for the jaguar. Your people burn
and the monkeys, plants, and toucans can't return.
Where are now the trees that drank the greenhouse gas?

They're burning into carbon and monoxide
to make room for farms that last a year or two,
then abandoned for more burning to a waste as wide
as the Amazon river blindness and as true

as planting one for ten cut down will tell
that planet earth warms to a burning hell.

When the Amazonian rainforests burn
and pump their tons of CO_2 into
the overburdened atmosphere we learn
that not only seven billion trees and plants are gone

that would have gladly drunk a ton or two
of the yearly multiplying excess CO_2
but exponentially the climate change raises the stakes.
Will Holland and Florida drown before we wake?

And will the Midwest grain fields die in drought
before enough people bother to figure out
what all the alarms and warnings are about,
and it's too late to grow the trees we need.

Those over fifty will die before that day,
but the younger ones will have to pay and pay.

SONNET 2

He that sitteth in the heavens shall laugh:
the Lord shall have them in derision.
                    Psalm 2:4 KJV

O how can I endure the daily evils
Of Republicans and their crazy president?
O how survive the sight of lying devils
Tricking the unthinking ignorant.

O how can I stay tears as billionaires
Take control to increase their wealth, our woe?
And how drive out the demons of despair,
And how defeat this frightening overthrow?

God sends comedians to make us laugh,
To lighten up our spirits, restore our hopes
That this too, soon shall pass and powerful riff-raff
Will be unmasked, unclothed, and seen as dopes,

Derided and deprived their powerful rule
By jabs of jokes, a knock out for each fool.

SONNET 14 (ALSO 53)

> *The fool hath said in his heart*
> *There is no God.*
>   *Psalm 14:1a KJV*

His name was Dennis, and he was such a fool.
He cobbled his religion from ad hoc sources.
He trashed his martyred wife whom he divorces
after she gave him all; he was so cruel.

He told a professor atheism's cool,
but just for the sake of argument, of course,
(I was there to witness that discourse)
he said as though he handed out a jewel,

"Okay, I will grant you that God exists."
The prof, who had once been a priest, then cried,
"Oh, this great gift! He grants me God exists!"
for Dennis had no power to grant what mind
should recognize, heart know. The prof then sighed,
rose, thrust his butt at Dennis, put him behind.

SONNET 22

My God, why hast thou forsaken me?
Why art thou so far from helping me, and
From the words of my roaring?
                              Psalm 22:1 KJV

My friend and I are seated at the back
On the main floor of Lyric Opera House.
A wall of lights onstage too bright, attack
Our eyes in sync with electric drums that douse

Our ears in wanton ignorance of the fact
The building's made to enlarge the human voice,
But now the lyrics are drowned in the deafening crack
Of rock music's electric guitar's gross-out noise.

It stops, and we see Jesus at the back
Of a dark stage, spotlighted on the cross.
The music whispers as the saddening black
surrounds the anguished cry and our sobbing pathos.

Thunder and strobe lights gone with stilled guitar.
It's the close of Webber and Rice's *Superstar*.

SONNET 23

> *Surely goodness and mercy shall follow me all the days*
> *of my life: and I will dwell in the house of the Lord for ever.*
> *Psalm 23:6 KJV*

I believe all accounts of near death experiences
with the encompassing love and bright colors,
the tales of heaven's glories filling the senses,
the meetings with loved ones, fathers and mothers.
But details will vary since each mansion's census
is different and unique for each soul that enters,
and the welcoming hands, embraces and kisses
come just from those loved and the lovers.
Those who come back from hell have to tell
a different life-changing story that scares,
of crying "Why am I here? I don't want to dwell
in this empty nightmare where no one cares.
Send me back! Send me back! And I will
change and serve God, love my neighbor,
work for peace, and lift the lives of the poor."

SONNET 26

> *Gather not my soul with sinners,*
> *nor my life with bloody men:*
> *in whose hands is mischief...*
>   *Psalm 26:9-10a KJV*

Now may my dwelling be in quilts and poems,
in prayers and sacred songs. May I rise up
with sacred choirs singing all the morns
of all my life. May I my home clean up
to be as fragrant as my flowers and trees that sup
the stormy rains. May all who think me warm
and open, an easy mark, a naïve dope,
be thwarted in their designs and cons, disarmed
divinely, and transformed to thy cause and quest.
May communities be cleansed and full of song.
May all people pull together and give their best
to build a loving world where all belong,
comforted and healed and free of sin,
like quilts and poems and prayers and songs to Him.

SONNET 29

> *The voice of the Lord is upon the waters: the God of glory thundereth: the Lord is upon many waters.*
> *Psalm 29:3 KJV*

Good news from Colorado's Gunnison
River in Black Canyon National Park.
It's all about the rainbow trout's remark-
able comeback from a population
crash caused by early starvation
brought on by a parasite's disease attack
deforming growth when trout are young.
The surprising discovery in an upriver section
that contained some immune rainbow trout sparked
a fish breeding program to reintroduce
the immune trout offspring back into the rivers.
The fishermen who flock when fishing's in season
can't keep the rainbows till they reproduce
enough numbers to satisfy wildlife givers
who labored to bring about their resurrection.

SONNET 31

> *Into thine hand I commit my spirit;*
> *Thou hast redeemed me, O Lord God of truth.*
> *Psalm 31:5 KJV*

Betrayal, mocking, scourging, nailing to a cross,
and Jesus cries out to God, and rightly so
that first line of Psalm twenty-two. and oh
God must have answered, regained His trust,

for then he quotes another line, this one
from Psalm thirty-one, not so well known,
although the line sure is, and free on loan
if you have need of it. One size fits anyone.

It's rather like elastic, not a belt,
that like a boxing fight, will go by rounds,
but like suspenders, up and down, surrounds.
Lift it to God, and let the misery melt.

The body and spirit are combined, but part
when death like truth comes in and stops your heart.

SONNET 36

O Lord, thou preservest man and beast.
Psalm 36:6c KJV

Noah marched in the animals two by two
In the huge ark he built to save some of all
Before the earth flooded from forty days of rainfall
As God had commanded Noah to do.

God's wrath at the evil ways people turn to
Won't be water this time but earth will turn a hot ball,
When ice melts and land dries and the oceans cook all
Life that dies mid rocks when the warnings come true.

The big money doubters with their powerful fist
Call in their experts to calculate risks
And other life is expendable, too bad, tsk-tsk,
And they slam it down hard on the endangered list.

How can our hearts grow the hearts of those shitters
So we all can make space for ourselves and God's critters?

SONNETS 42

> *Deep calleth unto deep at the noise of thy waterspouts:*
> *all thy waves and thy billows are gone over me.*
> *Psalm 42:7 KJV*

Our life begins as fish in a womb-sized sea
much like the ancient sea from which fish crawled
upon the land where fish to man evolved.
This unkind kind with greatest brain won't see

how dead red tides from ocean dumping fouled
these living waters that fed him clean and free
once, these garbaged waters that now plea
with dying dolphins, poisoned shellfish culled

from deadly toxic bays and estuaries,
sea turtles choked on plastic bags and things
mistook for jellyfish, muzzled, starved sea
lions with noses poked in nets and rings.

Fin-rot, ulcers, holes burned in lobsters tell
of man-made chemicals in a man-made hell.

Dear God, is there a way to save the seas?
A way to stop the dumping and pollution?
A way to clean the bays and estuaries?
And keep them clean. What is your best solution?

Kill man(un)kind in a blazing retribution?
Or let him kill himself with PCBs,
and the other toxic wastes in earth and ocean,
and then give back the earth to the lower species.

Let not this judgment fall so hard on man.
May your mercy fill his heart with loving care
for all your creatures. Make his ways so fair
that earth becomes the garden it began.

Wash up man's act before he's all washed up,
and global suicide's his poisoned cup.

SONNET 46

> *There is a river, the streams whereof*
> *shall make glad the city of God.*
> *Psalm 46:4a KJV*

What river is this river? I ask you.
Is it the Ohio, or the Rio Grande?
Perhaps some inner river I can't view,

a spirit that runs through my mind unplanned,
spontaneous, from unseen streams that dance
around the rocks and stones, over the sand.

Do earthquakes, hurricanes, happen by chance?
No, God's a great river of spiritual strength
and streams His messages of peace and plants

a refuge and a help that spans the length
of days through desolation and despair;
all wars and troubles, losses are a tenth

of any power to worry us, and gone
within the stillness that awaits His song.

SONNET 55

> *And I said, oh that I had wings like a dove!*
> *For then would I fly away, and be at rest.*
> *Psalm 55:6 KJV*

Here in the midst of war and suffering
that fills the T-V news and newspapers
with street crime, senseless murders, everything,
disease and sorrow, the cancer-causing vapors
of radiation, smog, poisons becoming
a scourge from the greedy rich in skyscrapers
with their deluded minions daily devising
profits to foul the earth and sea, landscapers
of destruction, death, beyond imagining.

Here in all this, I often want escape,
to fly like my pet dove up in a tree,
and though I called and called, I could but gape
in frantic loss as he chose liberty.
This world is not my home, the hymnist sings.
My body like his cage, empty, when I get wings.

SONNET 56

> *For thou hast delivered my soul from death: wilt not thou deliver my feet from falling, that I may walk before God in the light of the living.*
> *Psalm 56:13 KJV*

To write this poem I count the metric feet,
And I ask God to make the message stand,
So that its meaning may walk hand in hand
With light from living words and sonnet beat.

To write this poem I meditate, repeat
The words above to help me understand
The way that I must walk, not fall and land
Into the undertow, so I entreat

And plead you keep me upright, balanced,
Baptized in all waters I may wade
Although polluted, toxic, full of waste,
And poisoned dying fish in plastic made
To throw away. I pray let me not taste
The bitter brine of oil-drenched nonchalance.

SONNET 58

> *the righteous shall rejoice when he seeth*
> *the vengeance: he shall wash his feet*
> *in the blood of the wicked.*
> *Psalm 58:10 KJV*

Oh, Mueller and the FBI, you're slow.
I hope to heaven that you overthrow
this hacked election dictated by the foe.

Their poison was like a poisonous serpent's spears;
wise charmers' voices fell on deaf adder's ears.
Break the Russian hackers' teeth that tears

apart democracy. Wash them away
with revealed facts, continuously spray
on snails melting under truth's sun ray.

Be like a whirlwind that sweeps the land!
Empty the chamber pots and dirtied hand!
Bring down, bury corruption beneath its sand!

Oh, may the rule of law be fair with force,
and all the good and righteous will rejoice.

SONNET 60

> *Thou hast made the earth to tremble; thou hast broken it;*
> *heal the branches thereof for it shaketh, that had shewed*
> *the people hard things . . .*
> *Psalm 60:2-3a KJV*

Earthquakes shake Hawaii and Japan. The sea
roils with blasts of missile tests off coasts
of North Korea. Plastic straws, debris,
disable fish and seabirds while Trump boasts
that he makes the world safe but tears apart
long time alliances with friendly nations
and courts the foes that easily outsmart
him and strive to rule our country, like the Russians
fracture the world and our nation. Lord, replant
the trees of life in deeper, richer soil
by turning our mistaken citizens
from folly into seeing truth, recant
harmful allegiances, turn round and toil
to make all lives worth living for all persons.

SONNET 71

*Deliver me, O my God, out of the hand of the wicked,
out of the hand of the unrighteous and cruel man.*
Psalm 71:4 KJV

Even beauty and much wealth cannot keep you
safe from clever, crafty men's cruel trap
that plunders, takes your body and your true
sense of self-worth, and makes you feel like crap.

So if you're old and ugly, poor, disabled,
what are your chances if you're the female sex
not to be robbed by any white man now tattooed
upon his forehead sixty-six point six.

Those who know the book of Revelation's word
know what that string of numbers signifies.
Still that leaves of the white male vote a third
Who, seeing the better man was woman, voted wise.

She would have won but for hate-fueled ignorance,
Russian meddling, sex and race prejudice.

SONNET 82

> *How long will ye judge unjustly and accept the persons of the wicked? Defend the poor and fatherless: do justice to the afflicted and needy . . . rid them out of the hand of the wicked.*
>
> *Psalm 82:2-4b KJV*

A nightmare's become real in our fair land.
We were a model of democracy.
White male dominance and tyranny
has dumped a granite boot of greed's command
on citizens whose votes are nullified
by gerrymandering the districts and
the electoral college in a poisoned tide
of oil, carbon gasses, and concrete sand.
The climate prophets are now persecuted.
The president now wants to rule like kings
with power absolute who lied and looted
the people like past peasant underlings.
We need to rise again in revolution!
We need to write a better Constitution!

SONNET 89

> *Thou hast a mighty arm; strong is thy hand,*
> *and high is thy right hand. Justice and judgment*
> *are the habitation of thy throne: mercy and truth*
> *shall go before thy face.*
>
> *Psalm 89:13-14 KJV*

Today I praise the manliness of helpful men,
because this Friday 13th I was in a pickle
after mistaking what was a pedestrian
opening in a curb for car-width I clunked
my front wheels over the curb, and I was stuck,
not able to go back or forth. What then?
A man saw what had happened, and bad luck
turned good for as he pondered the front end
and how to lift it up to get the car
back over the curb, three helpful men joined him.
The strength of four white men I did not care
to know just how they voted then performed
this awesome act of rescue because when
this needed to be done, it needed men.

SONNET 91

> *He shall cover thee with his feathers, and under his wings*
> *shalt thou trust; his truth shall be thy shield and buckler.*
> *Psalms 91:4 KJV*

What's left of all the dinosaurs who thundered
bodacious bodies before the mammals came
in tiny horse and woolly mammoth herds?
The descendants of the dinosaurs became
the light and winged creatures we call birds.
From giant lizards we got loons, some claim.
Sparrows, owls, hawks, eagles, wrens, and songbirds,
flamingoes, turkeys, geese evolved the same.
If brontosaurus whose fossils fill whole rooms
begot the hummingbird, why then what doom
is death? Extinction is evolution's sieve,
what of creation dies and what will live.
So earthly bodies sink like dinosaurs
their bones in bogs, and their winged spirit soars.

SONNET 96

> *Let the field be joyful, and all that is therein:*
> *then shall all the trees of the wood rejoice*
> *before the LORD; for he cometh, for he cometh*
> *to judge the earth . . .*
>
> *Psalms 96:12 KJV*

Snow frosted Douglas firs in silence stand,
forms softened by the fog's November morn.
Round the ancient trunks of sequoias grand,
the soul finds refuge from the chainsaw's groan.

When a young man, Paul Rokich, saddened, planned
beneath the clear-cut desolate Utah mountains
to make them green again. A hundred thousand
acres with thousands of thousand trees are bird reborn.

So I plant acorns to give the oaks my hand
and write the Senate to give the trees a horn
whose leaves but whisper to hearts that understand
our connections to the squirrels, oaks, and acorns.

Divine green spirit, help us plant and care
to reap a greener, more song-filled, clean-air year.

SONNET 107

> *He poureth contempt upon princes, . . .*
> *Yet setteth he the poor on high from affliction,*
> *And maketh him families like a flock.*
> *Psalm 107:40-41 KJV*

There's never sufficient reason to despair.
Though dunces, scoundrels be voted to high office,
though poor and homeless huddle everywhere,
though hypocrisy and lies mask power's malice,
though dreams dissolve like sulfur in the air,
and rain their bitter disappointed dust
to acid etch the soul beyond repair,
though hard-won gains be trashed by cruel and callous
so-called public servants, yet every hair
is numbered, and each faint hope that hops
with lagomorphic life leaps Fred Astaire
like, dancing a delight of growing gallops.
A pitied pecked plucked bird can sing and fly
when God's love tunes the throat and strings the sky.

SONNET 123 BLUES

Our Lord is exceedingly filled with the scorning of those that are at ease, and with contempt of the proud,
Psalm 123:4 KJV

Those who have been elected to our Congress,
Those representatives voted to Congress,
Care not for voters but their own largess.

All the lies by cabinet appointees,
The looting by the cabinet appointees,
Does sabotage the services they seize.

The people have been scorned by government,
The citizens get contempt from government,
And tweets of lies come from the president.

People who can discern and know the facts,
Reporters who find out the real facts,
Are sick at soul reporting evil acts.

Can even the FBI cast out those knaves?
Or must we suffer and endure like slaves?

SONNET 126

Turn again our captivity, O Lord, as the streams
in the south. They that sow in tears shall reap in joy.
Psalm 126:4-5 KJV

Today we drove to Guadalupe River,
Where its streams flow slow on stones of clay.
There three white ducks swam back and forth, as never
I could recall I'd seen so bright a day.

We walked a ways upstream and saw again
A trinity, three gray Egyptian geese,
Their bright eyes ringed with black just like the men
In ancient Egypt outlined eyes with kohl grease.

Another wonder was a butterfly,
A black-veined orange gulf fritillary.

And then into the stream three Texas deer
Did prance their dainty hooves full of delight.
We stood transfixed because they came so near,
Then watched them go in trees and out of sight.

SONNET 136

> *To him which smote great kings for his mercy endureth for ever.*
> *And slew famous kings for his mercy endureth for ever.*
> *Psalm 136:17-18 KJV*

We sorely need good leadership on earth.
We need more people empowered everywhere.
Intelligence and knowledge, such a dearth!
We need wise leaders who will care and share.

Our president and Putin need be replaced,
The dictator of North Korea, too.
Congress and the Senate are disgraced,
Corrupted by wealthy leaders who undo

Every good and lawful benefit
For all that live in these United States.
The lies, delusions, greed, and every bit
Of demonizing good must dissipate.

Dear God, I pray You change, bring down, recall,
So that Your mercy may endure for all.

SONNET 137

> *By the rivers of Babylon, there we sat down, yes,*
> *we wept, when we remembered Zion.*
> *We hung our harps upon the willows in the midst thereof.*
> *How shall we sing the Lord's song in a strange land?*
>   *Psalm 137:1-2,4 KJV*

I wept at the November election's's loss,
for Donald Trump had hijacked Lincoln's party,
or what it had become, unfortunately,
a woman, immigrant hating, racist chaos.

My land was ruled now by a billionaire boss,
a lying, swindling, parasitic bully,
who, using Hitler's playbook craftily
had put good public servants on a cross.

Now I must pledge allegiance to the theft
of fair elections, health care, clean air, life
secure from excess capitalism's curse;
and I must sing the national anthem now bereft
of safeguards from gun violence and needless strife.
The constant lies and crimes are getting worse.

SONNET 138

> *Though I walk in the midst of trouble, thou wilt revive me:*
> *thou shalt stretch forth thine hand against the wrath*
> *of mine enemies, and thy right hand shall save me.*
> *Psalm 138:7 KJV*

Hard work and sacrifice are not enough.
The world today is too political.
Too many managers make tasks too tough.
They use the stress of no-win to enthrall
with power to enslave, make life so rough
that all suffer at their whim and maul.
And if you have the nerve to call their bluff
the nasty game it is, to have that gall,
then you will pay the bitter price, and God
alone can save you from their wrath. But yet
impotence can be the power of the odd,
and to walk away can mark you as a prophet.
The truest measure of a man of power
is how he treats those under: do they flower?

SONNET 139

> *Whither shall I go from thy spirit? Whither shall I flee from thy presence? If I ascend up into heaven thou art there.*
> *If I make my bed in hell, behold, thou art there. If I say, surely the darkness shall cover me, even the night shall be made light about me . . . the darkness and the light are both alike to thee.*
> *Psalms 139:7- 8,11-12c KJV*

In the beginning light and dark were good,
like yin and yang, two parts to make a whole,
for each defined the other as contrast should.

And when did dark become the evil dole?
A function of the fall from innocence?
Redemption then restores dark's rightful role.

The quilt *Sunshine and Shadow* represents
that all is good when love is in control
and fills its artful place in immanence.

A white dove and a black swan paint your soul,
rainbows of birds and flowers, colors that laud
creation's gift; joys light and dark unroll.

With love His Son for us survived the rod,
so no dark cliff, white wall, keeps us from God.

SONNET 142

> *Teach me to do thy will: for thou art my God: thy spirit is good: lead me into the land of uprightness. Quicken me, O Lord, for thy name's sake: for thy righteousness' sake bring my soul out of trouble.*
> *Psalm 142:10-11 KJV*

There is much sorrow here and everywhere,
so I am cautioned not to watch the news
by those who do not want me to despair
but take my mind off what I cannot choose
but to grieve over troubled with much care
for tragedies I have no power to use
that would prevent, undo, make right, repair
great damage and destruction to what glues
people together. I am here, not there,
and it is summer; I am too blessed for blues.
It is enough for me to do and share
with what I have and can and so refuse
to be downhearted when plants are green
and flowering, but be happy and serene.

SONNET 146

> *Happy is he . . . whose hope is in the Lord his God*
> *which made heaven, and earth, the sea, and all*
> *that therein is: which keepeth truth for ever:*
> *Psalm 146 :5,6 KJV*

The news is not all bad. Today there was a story
on WGN about a strange bronze statue
of Jesus and its journey of marine glory
to stand only underwater for the view
of deep sea divers off of Florida's coast.
It was the desire of an Italian sculptor
to place the holy presence of Jesus Christ
with his arms raised in saving rapture
among the fishes, sea urchins, and coral reefs.
It was discovered, found by divers
down underwater stirring their beliefs,
who pulled it up on land to clean, deliver
to Chicago, and there displayed until
returned to where it had been made to dwell.

'Christ of the Abyss
Beverley Rose Enright

SONNET 150

> *Praise him with the sound of a trumpet... psaltery and harp... string instruments and organs... Praise ye the Lord.*
>
> *--Psalm 150:3-4b.6b KJV*

Around us moves an unseen lace of love
Most vivid in our childhood's wondering awe
When hearts are small and soft as a kitten's paw,
What most people have but a memory of.
Around us hums this harmony of love,
Unheard amidst the traffic and the noise
That hurts our ears and blasts away our joys,
But it can cover like a furry glove,
If we but still our mind and empty be,
Like woodwinds waiting for a blowing burst
That starts the skillful touch so much rehearsed,
That bows the strings and presses piano keys
To release the singing voice that praising swells
And moves the hands that shake the ringing bells.

from ONE HUNDRED SONNETS TO THE CALCULUS

I. THE GIFT OF A TEXT FULL OF ERRORS

> *What math gives students is certainty.*
> Yoram Sagher

We don't have to pay to buy this text
because we'll pay in other ways, in loss
of trust and faith, confused, puzzled, perplexed,
unsure of answers when the answers given

are incorrect, so that the muddled mess
becomes a mystery of hell and heaven,
a passion play of curves and tangents flexed
to solve by finding limits to counteract

the gift of a family full of errors, yes,
and the gift of a world full of errors, tares
sown among the grain and cut *en masse*
as the text is grasped by mind and heart that cares

to differentiate the curves of fate
and integrate the love beneath the hate.

IV. THE REMOVABLE DISCONTINUITY

A tiny circle interrupts the line.
A value makes the fraction undefined.
It is the missing data and the sign

that leads us to the subtlety of form
God serves us in His riddled arrows firm
pointing to the little holes "forlorn"

the very word that like a bell called Keats
to pour into his urn of metric beats
the sweat beads on his fevered body's heat.

The Spirit comes, called, desired, or unbidden
to close the discontinuity, the hidden
hole in the whole lifeline. The soul smitten

yearns to remove discontinuities, though hard
for what is impossible is possible with God.

V. THE PINCHING THEOREM

She pinched a petal and pierced a petal with it
As my silver butterfly blonde angel said,
"You must share your suffering, not hide it."
My wee brush touched a petal's detail on wood.

All life is open at both ends and meets
In the instant needle's pinch as a quilt is stitched
To pull the quilt's three layers together tight,
The top we appliqué the face that greets

The world, and a soft batt between the bottom sheet
Seems to disappear so snugly bound,
That very stitch, the now, that puts the neat
Stay-in-place to hold together the loose bond.

When we take the limit closing near to none,
The cyclic cross of Christ in three is one.

VI. LEIBNIZ'S DERIVATIVE WITH RESPECT TO DESCARTES'S CROSS RELIGIOUSLY

God is no respecter of persons. His call
Speaks forth inside the lowest, highest, middest,
In the midst of any doing, mighty, middling, or small.
Plans and dreams are radically and ratio-ly recast.

Leibniz's derivative notation, one under all,
Could be one as a cross, a yes, or test
Or any to be derived. I think of Saul
Blinded by light going to Damascus.

I think of Moses and the burning bush that spoke
"I am." "Not me, O Lord, I have a stutter."
Or Samuel waked by a voice that was no joke,
hallucination, but a command, no dreamy mutter.

Obey, rise up, be nailed to Calvary's cross
before Easter's dawning ratio of gain and loss.

VII. LEIBNIZ'S DERIVATIVE WITH RESPECT TO DESCARTES'S CROSS PHILOSOPHICALLY

If there exists within each soul a primitive force
When modified to some determinate motion
Becomes the derivative force in the course
Of the monad's development and perceptions
Such that each unity mirrors the universe
And fulfills itself, unless hindered, will dance
In a harmonious system, but also can reverse,
Be passive, a feature Leibniz called prime substance,
Pure only in God, but in created monadic substance
Is limited, prone to "passions" of confused perceptions,
The points depending in the bar of separation;
The ratio of point to point, d cross notation
Is Leibniz's dogwood blossom of decision.

VIII. RULES OF POWER, POLYNOMIAL, PRODUCT, AND QUOTIENT

We can't forget the chain, the chain of minds
around the globe studying calculus.
Newton and Leibniz live, and that reminds
how history lives in the retelling to us.

All knowledge is not historical, Croce.
The bounds of senses, reason, accepted wisdom,
omit that which confounds, a piercing eye
of God whose intersection shows the kingdom.

The world we think is real and rely
steadfastly on becomes as just the smoke
spent from the crematory pyre. We fly,
new wings released, sprung from the mental yoke

by power rules that make the burdens light
like easy slumbers of a summer's night.

X. IMPLICIT DIFFERENTIATION

The equation for an ellipse is not a function, but
Tangents exist, a cross of thorns, at all points
On the non-functional line and jut
Their differentials implicitly in their joints.
When y equals zero, dy over dx is undefined.
What is defined is a vertical line that drops
From the naked body nailed
Where faith crosses history and stops
Time, mind, memory, and endeavor.
The ellipse's equation is a relation, and implicit
In that is two y values, plus and minus,
For what goes up must come down except
beyond gravity's limit. What comes down may
go up. Cosine derivative redeems, $-\sin(xy)$.

XII. SET THE DERIVATIVE EQUAL TO ZERO TO GET THE MAX AND MIN

What is the minimum energy needed to remove
Cheaply, efficiently, the salt from the sea?
Then would deserts blossom, give fruit to feed
Those starving in Africa, India, South America?

Then would Texas be saved from dunes of dust
After the Ogallala aquifer is gone?
And give the Colorado back to the Navajo,
Once well-fed farmers, now welfare drunks?

Land is cleared, trees cut down, and desert comes.
People move on, but the desert follows them.
Oh to draw water from the sea as from a well
Like where Jesus gave the woman living water.

What's the maximum resources, time needed to pay
To find a cheap way to drink the sea, if there be a way?

XXIV. THE MEAN VALUE THEOREM FOR INTEGRALS

Elegant like art and poetry, this math
is still ever practical and turns a buck
as art and poems shine sunbeams on a duck
as it takes flight from lakes and makes its path
across clouds of emotions and the sunset's track
red of the heart to light as from a heavenly host
of angels and saints of nature's bounty, the clack
of tongue and typewriter yet to be lost
and found anew in the perfect dance,
the journey with significance primary.
With math, it's secondary to the prance
of algorithmic matters mercenary.
What's the value? What does it mean and be
To integrate math with art and poetry?

XXVI. AREA BETWEEN TWO CURVES: WALKING ON WATER AT THE VOLO BOG

To compute the area of the pond in the bog,
first find the functions that shape the edge,
then use the definite integral, coordinates to log
what function to subtract between to gauge

the area of wood to step on above the sog-
gy peat that slowly sinks beneath the ledge
of Styrofoam so as to walk in fog
on water from the past above the sinking sedge

with eyes upon a vision seen through smog
in winds that chill the feet with despair's sledge
driving down who stands in doubt. But jog
in faith through tamaracks that hedge

the area inside the bog, then God
with arms of curves joins two trunks of nods.

XXIX. THE SURFACE AREA OF WORLD WITHOUT END

> *When He said, "Be perfect," He meant it. He meant that we must go in for the full treatment. It is hard, but the sort of compromise we are all hankering after is harder—in fact, it is impossible. It may be hard for an egg to turn into a bird: it would be a jolly sight harder for it to learn to fly by remaining an egg. We are like eggs at present. And you cannot go on indefinitely being just an ordinary, decent egg. We must be hatched or go bad.*
>
> C. S. Lewis, *Mere Christianity*

Imagine the globe rotating on its poles
like on an axis of the cross of Descartes
and find the area of the function of the soul
that penetrates life's thickness to the heart
of this globe and integrates like Lowell's
"Vision of Sir Launfal", at the start
June's knight and beggar, then at the close
of the calendar's circle, for both are part
of the turning world like a ten-ton ball
swings to wreck the hopes and dreams and art
of love. The mortar, glass, and bricks, the goals
fall from standing steel girders of Christ's heart.
If we all live an integrated life
We spare the global surface from waste and strife.

XXXII. TRANSLATION PRINCIPLE AND FINDING THE SLOPE OF A LINE TANGENT TO A CURVE AT A POINT

to Robert Gethner

in memoriam: Marc Chagall (1888 - 1985)

We meet again at the exhibit of Chagall's
Works on Paper at the Art Institute of Chicago.
You shake hands with my husband whose own style
of teaching, that bouncing dance and open throw
of explication, lithe lank antelope
like grace and concentration. From Kant
to calculus, from the Order's songs to slopes
goes the transference from his life to yours.
Your chalk turned pink and pale green,
colored pastels of curves and lines Chagall
used to form his lovers, cocks, and violins,
floral bouquets, red angels, blue fish, all
line, curve, color to kiss the heart and eye;
above calculus, his forms float and limits fly.

XXXVI. CONTINUOUS FUNCTIONS

*And other sheep I have which are not of this fold:
and they shall hear my voice, and there shall be
one fold, and one shepherd.*
                                John 10:16 KJV

I place my mind in a Hindu heaven this time
since God has turned my feet now in that way
and put me in this ashram for what rhyme
or reason poetic in function as each day
continues the song of the day before; as each limit
brings, or doesn't; as every life brings, say,
birth, youth, adulthood, death, unless cut off by crime
or accident, if a greater function overlay
the lesser one. One great continuous line
runs through all of us and yesterday
is connected and differentiable by design
to an infinity of primes like rays
from the sun or source of cosmic energy
to lift up an untouchable like me.

XXXVII. PROOFS OF THE LIMIT LAWS

If given an egg of epsilon that's more
Than zero and a delta greater too,
So zero is less than the absolute
Value does imply that the Big Fix

Upon the cross is less than epsilon
For eggshells suffer badly stones and sticks,
And even for an eggshell Hamlet groaned
Soliloquizing at the frenzied Fates

Our destinies and visions drive us to
Take arms against a sea of hiding hell,
And by opposing dive a drowning fool,
And O Horatio, what I could tell

Of limit less than let it break and be;
Not boiled enough, the yoke swims silently.

XLI. THE NUPTIAL NIGHT OF THE COROLLARIES: CONSEQUENCES OF THE MEAN VALUE THEOREM

If the derivative's zero, the function's constant,
A constant like the white lace of the sea
As it throws upon the rock its filmy billows,
The gown of the bride of Christ, the constant C.

Christ now is a radiant sun in a gold shirt
And a smile that beams on all benevolently,
A dear dark face and chalking hands that glow
And show equal derivatives f and g.

This calculus teacher to me is heaven sent;
Even primed equal to the other, he differs though
In the constant C or K which can with either go,
But K like kindness makes this one different.

Help me overcome my failure's scars.
Set it to zero, dark face full of stars.

XLIII. THE CHAIN RULE

To derive a function that fits inside another
function is to derive the outer function first
and multiply that times the inner one
and again for each more inside function

until the inmost inner is derived.
The global is the outermost, the size
of all human societies alive
containing nations that contain the ties

of ethnic groups, political collections,
religions, towns and families, each one
derived to find the tangents' touch, connections
to clasp the heart's concentric will to come

in time before the guns go off, bombs dropped.
The rule is first the world, the hating stopped.

XLV. DERIVATIVES OF SINES AND COSINES

How well they go together; how they change
into each other when derived again and again
with higher and higher derivation; true

love couldn't be more empathetic to do
such exchanging and role reversal, to descend
even to negatives as the derivations range

to higher powers. Would that we in others' shoes
could so see ourselves as the soul ascends
in this turning, burning, spiraling arranger

of divine rebirth. Like two sides of a coin,
like day and night, joy and sorrow, the change
of seasons, the tides, rotations that never end.

God's eternal love cycles the Son,
the circle sines and cosines square to one.

XLVI. ASYMPTOTES; INFINITE LOVE INCREASES WITHOUT BOUND AROUND THE WHEEL OF FAITH

In studying math, am I just trying to stuff
a square peg in a round hole? This can
be done if the circle's radius is one-half
the diagonal of the square. If you begin
with a unit circle inscribed in a triangle,
then a square inscribed inside the circle, again
a circle inside the square, then a pentagon
inside the circle, another circle, then a hexagon,
and on and on, what is the limit? Guess.
The center? A point vanishing on the horizon?
No. Calculus yields a limit exact as radius
of a circle one-twelfth the radius of circle one.
The series ends with infinite sides of the final
polygon and its circle identical.

L. ANTIDERATIVES

We can, like Dorothy, go to Oz with derivation
and come back home with antiderivation.
For every trip inside, there is reverse,
a formula back, click heels, recite verse.
There is a difference though between deriving
and antideriving. A function has one only
derivative, but that non-function has unending
antiderivatives because of the constant C,
the Christ, for when we go tangent to life
in God, we come back the same way, altered
by the change of C. Constants are not wife
to a function as it travels between worlds.
You lose your constant when you go. You gain
abundant life constants when you return.

LII. RIEMANN SUMS AND THE INTEGRAL

From Henry David Thoreau to Gandhi to
Martin Luther King, the sums of saints
stacked vertically, measures the area through
which the slim soul squeezes its ascent.
If "all that rises does converge" in a
continuous function for which exists an integral
like a narrow door, then strait the holy gate
and high, though wide the sacred heart for all
the Riemann sums of spreading communion toll
church bells of salvation, safety in a great
Good Shepherd's care; not the demons of hell
or their burning taunts and smoking guns of hate
can change the right solution, nonviolence
of right thought: "God is Good" brings paradise.

LV. AREA BETWEEN TWO CURVES

In an Edward Weston photo of a nude
Cropped with care at waist and knee, you spy
A function $y = f(x)$ to caress the back
And a function $y = g$(string of x) to caress the thigh.

Then you can now explore and integrate
The area between two curves, subtract
What lies below from what's above intact
Between the left and right bounds of the portrait.

Beyond the photo comes a number of sighs
To move you to translate and calculate
The mastication of cuisine that lies
There now transformed to another taste and state.

O come into this sad heart, tongue the swerves
Of fingers on the functions' shape between two curves.

LVI. VOLUME OF A SOLID OF REVOLUTION: DISK METHOD, OR EZEKIEL SAW THE WHEEL

If we double the functions and then spin
Them around Descartes's cross with one inside
The other, you inside me, your thumb within
My fingers, or the birdsong that airy rides

Through the doughnut's hole as we slice a thin
Washer from the middle, watch it glide
Through sums and limits. The formula begins
With pi in the face and ends with "why hide"

Enclosing the difference between the two in grins,
And multiplying each one by itself to abide
By all the rules, and if not, then by God all sin
Transforms to a vision of whirling wheels, but Brother died.

The riddle of his death is the volume odd
When faith is added to the spinning grace of God.

LVII. VOLUME OF A SOLID OF REVOLUTION: SHELL METHOD, OR TED KOOSER'S "ONION WOMAN" REVISITED

To get a view of the Riemann sums of shells,
Slice off an onion's ends and slide the rings
Apart and add the volume of each to tell
How a life is wrapped and trapped in strings.

I used to layer clothing, cover like shells
And walls, like fences for protection, like fur
On animals, like cages at the zoo, like prison cells.
It's easier at times to find cylinders than washers.

Better to protect than clean a mess when bells
Of Edgar Allan Poe start ringing. One cylinder
Is really all you need for faerie dells,
Angel song, rainbows, the integrator

Of warring factions that mimic in the heart
The warring nations that pull the world apart.

LXVIII. DERIVATIVES AND INTEGRALS OF INVERSE TRIGONOMETRIC FUNCTIONS

In memoriam: Eugene Ormandy (1899-1985)

But Love has pitched his mansion in
The place of excrement.
    William Butler Yeats,
     "Crazy Jane Talks with the Bishop"

To fit the definition of a function
That switches values from the x to the y axis,
Shape the inverse curves like sweeping wings,

The wings of swans in Wagner's *Lohengrin*
When Ormandy conducts the Bridal Chorus
And the Mormon Tabernacle Choir sings

in English. The Prelude to Act III (arcsin
Derivative) was Ormandy's top choice.
One over root of one minus square brings

Chad Meistersinger riding swans in motion
Of silver mind in metaphor of marriage
To integrate the roots of squares and differences,

An epithalamion to poetry and math;
A swan's guano grows the arc and cross of faith.

LXXI. BASIC INTEGRATION FORMULAS: TED KOOSER'S "A CHILD'S GRAVE MARKER"

The poets ever do it best; they go beyond
formulas and conventions memorized
to symbolize and image the universalized

particulars of the heart. The grandmother's
cast iron cake mold, the white plaster
lamb that goes "soft in the rain" of seventy years

at the lost girl's grave, melting like caked sugar
"in its own sweet time." The good eager
girl molded white by the cast iron grandmother,

but lamblike, so that the torrents of tears
wear her whiteness away like snow in April's rains,
the tragedies and sorrows of sad years.

Oh, Ted Kooser, to integrate it all exquisitely,
such beautiful love as ever man could give me!

LXXVI. DIVERGENCE AND THE DEATH OF CETACEANS: OIL SPILL AT PRINCE WILLIAM SOUND

> *"Humans are barbaric!" Paul told Jean-Paul.*
> *"I think I'd rather hang out with whales."*
> Rex Weyler, *The Song Of The Whale*

God's massive rulers of the seas, the whales
Die with the dolphins, birds, and fish for men
Who knew the better way but would not do it

But would dump their pollution near the site
Of whale communion, the Orca Lab; heroic tales
Paul Spong told of Greenpeace's work to ban

The killing and abuse of brother mammals
Blessed with bigger brains and wiser fit
To their environment. Like Christ, how can

Creatures live long whose song speaks to the pit
Of most of man(un)kind's murderous refusal
To learn and understand. Though Jonah ran

Into a whale before he raged God's question why,
How will it change men's hearts to sing and die?

LXXVIII. INFINITE SERIES AS A CIRCLE BETWEEN TWO FACING MIRRORS

Chardin saw evolution as a series
of diversifying species until a stage
of maximum proliferation; species
would then begin extinction and converge

ultimately becoming but one species
of Christ consciousness. The edge
or turn from this diverging to converge
was like a globe with alpha one-celled species

at the southern pole and most diversely
evolved at the equator. Life-forms would then
begin converging into a form like men
but rising to a spiritual supreme

he called omega, a planet's northern pole
where all of life transfigures into soul.

LXXIX. WHEN THERE'S NO ANTIDERIVATIVE FOR THE INTEGRAND F . . . AND THAT WORD WON'T DO EITHER

In memoriam, John Ciardi (1915 - 1986)

"but are earth creatures chosen by moon-pull
to live and flow––here no other word will do––
fuck one another forever if possible across the stars.
            Galway Kinnell, *"The Waking"*

"Love should intend realities. Goodbye."
            John Ciardi, *"Exit Line"*

I saw you once, *Divine Comedy* translator,
At a poets' panel at Kent State, the day
You criticized Leroi Jones for writing poems
On Dante's *Inferno* without ever having read Dante.

Then one of our black writers, Lloyd Weaver,
Jumped up yelling with the finger "Fuck Dante!" "Young man,
That is not proper discourse . . ." Angry, hurt,
You fought for civilization in a stuffed shirt.

Arra Garab told his students that Lloyd had dropped
A turd at a garden party; Bob Jackson, ever
Provoking, said, "Why didn't Ciardi, a poet,
Say, "Fuck you!' too?" Then where would it have stopped?

You were right, John, to flinch and fuss for fair.
"Fuck" deafs the ear; it's the jackhammer of despair.

LXXXIX. FINDING MYSELF DUSTY ON DERIVATIVES

Dear God, it has been close to twenty years.
I did not find time to review. I lose
The way arriving tardy full of fears
Because the school year ended with the muse
At work on troubled passions; fighting tears
I seat myself deep in discussing views
Of definitions only vaguely clear
Starting with instantaneous speed that moves
To approximating tangents with secant spears
Piercing parallel to the tangent's fuse
Like calculators do it. Then appears
The wings of the absolute value, this old news
Of the undefined derivative undoes
Confused anxiety and my heart cheers.

XCII. THE LOSS OF A PARTICULAR CONSTANT WHEN REVERSING: POWER RULE FOR DERIVATIVES AND ANTIDERIVATIVES

You can't go home again without a loss.
What once was clear, specific, and well-known
drops into mystery like milk in sauce.
You can't go back and get the milk alone,

or know it is not butter, flour, cheese,
but one of these, and so we mark it C,
or K if you are German, if you please.
It is a constant unspecifically.

If you translate this sonnet into French,
then back to English, you will see that words
have several synonyms whose meanings drench
with subtle changes, and the choice is blurred.

Going home you recognize the place,
but something's not the same in what you face.

XCVI. THE SANDWICH THEOREM IN A SQUEEZING PINCH BETWEEN A ROCK AND A HARD PLACE

When there's no room to wiggle or breathe deep,
Spread a thin layer of smooth peanut butter
On one slice of bread, top with another
To stick together, then vertically keep
Pressing hard the blunt edge of the knife
Without splitting the sandwich in two,
Then cut horizontally, part it to view
The horrible truth of my pain-filled life.
My sad function is pinched in between
Two other functions that seem to embrace,
And the value taken at that pinpoint space
Is the same as the two it's squeezed through,
Anorexically thin as this linear grace
Threaded between a rock and a hard place.

XCVIII. THE BRIDGE LINKING DIFFERENTIATION AND INTEGRATION: THE FUNDAMENTAL THEOREM OF CALCULUS

This gives to you two constants j and k,
with a continuous function in between,
like a suspension bridge is a grand way
connecting two communities and seen

to be a link rising across a strait
or river like the Brooklyn Bridge that spans
the Hudson, or the bridge called Golden Gate.
It's a sparkling clarity that stands and brands

into the brain this fundamental tie
that binds our hearts even if we divide
as differential parts that dumbly try
to break the spirit's tender bond that hides
and whispers of the fundamental truth
that we are all connected deep inside.

C. BLOWING KISSES TO RON COLEMAN AT THE KELVYN PARK HIGH SCHOOL RETIREMENT DINNER JUNE 2008

A tragic loss of sight keeps Ron at home,
and so he is not present here for us.
He who has given much and then excess
of much I know would greatly wish to come.

Well, I am here to honor this great man,
but can I make this sonnet integral,
a slice to fully measure all in all,
the volume of that vast accomplished sum?

It is too hard. My geometric very
limited poetic skills too dear
to see the way God sees that Ron is here,
the way the number i, imaginary,

raised to an even power becomes the real
man in us we love and deeply feel.

IN THE LAND OF THE EXTINCT BIRDS

REVISED AND EXPANDED

IN THE LAND OF THE EXTINCT BIRDS

a series of poems in forms

I fly in my wing chair
    fueled only with words
from two books to the land
    of the extinct birds.

I've my paint box and brushes,
    my colored pencils and papers,
my passions, fond wishes,
    from the land of skyscrapers.

I've come to the shore
    of this historical place
to see and explore
    what we cannot replace.

[NOTE: The books referred to in the first stanza are VANISHED SPECIES by David Day, London editions, 1981, and EXTINCT BIRDS, revised edition, by Errol Fuller, Cornell University Press, New York, 2001.]

ELEGY TO THE ELEPHANT BIRD

The largest bird that ever lived on earth
Endured millennia over thirty times
The duration of human existence's length
Protected by its size and tropic climes.

At ten feet tall, it weighed over half a ton.
Its massive legs, terrible talons, and beak
Shaped like a sword caused fear to look upon.
No predator but one though small and weak

Could threaten its dominion and it reigned,
The lords of Madagascar, until men
Entered its island forest home and aimed
Their capture at the eggs extinguishing them.

And oh! What eggs they were to startle sight!
The French and Dutch and Portuguese seamen
Of the sixteenth century eagerly sought
These curios to sell to merchantmen.

The circumference of these eggs could swallow up
Three times the eggs of the largest dinosaurs.
The yolk swam in nine liters; its omelet
Was more than sixteen dozen eggs of ours.

The birds retreated to the forest core
As burning, cutting, clearing musket bearers
Drove them into hiding from the shore,
Took eggs and habitat, the fatal errors.

Merchants and pirates care not to record,
To observe or preserve exotic birds,
And when their remotest last abode was gored,
Too late Gutenberg sent out the words.

The island of Madagascar is a tomb
For many extinct species, and its girth
Is witness to when men could not make room
For the largest birds that ever lived on earth.

Elephant Bird

Beverley Rose Enright

MEMORIUM TO THE MOA

The moas are all gone away.
Maori did not kill them all
tripping with slings of cords and balls
around their legs in deadly play.

The tallest birds that ever lived
hid in the islands of New Zealand
away from the exposing sand.
In thickest woods they yet conceived,

laying eggs to feed a tribe
of natives that buried a chief with one
sitting in his lap so lone
exhumed intact with chick inside.

They lasted fifty years beyond
the eighteenth century so that
an English scientist, in fact,
could study, write, and even send

reports and drawings, measurements
to awe the ornithologists.
The Royal Academy exists
to spread the news of such immense

rare and wingless birds to men
who care to read about such strange
creatures still alive to change
their worldview of kind and kin.

But settlers sinned and were too quick
for flocks of birds too thinned and shy
to procreate, and that is why
the naturalists could not protect.

And what is left for me to say?
Not even in the Royal Zoo
could some be shipped for public view.
The moas are all gone away.

A DIRGE FOR THE DODO

Three centuries, three centuries,
    And it will be centuries more,
The dodo means extinction,
    Lost relic of aging lore.

Fat and round and fifty pounds,
    And it will be centuries more,
The dodo had a massive beak,
    Lost relic of aging lore.

Naked head half veiled with fuzz,
    And it will be centuries more,
The dodo had small flightless wings,
    Lost relic of aging lore.

Diamond eyes and downy feathers,
    And it will be centuries more,
The dodo had a three plumed tail,
    Lost relic of aging lore.

Laid single eggs and swallowed stones,
    And it will be centuries more,
The largest pigeon that ever lived,
    Lost relic of aging lore.

Slaughtered by Dutch colonists,
    And it will be centuries more,
Who brought the rats that ate the eggs,
    Lost relic of aging lore.

It cooed its name dovelike and slow,
    And it will be centuries more,
A soft, maternal *doh-doh, doh-doh*,
    Lost relic of aging lore.

Three centuries, three centuries,
    And it will be centuries more,
The dodo means extinction,
    Lost relic of aging lore.

RONDEL FOR THE MAURITIUS RED HEN

Why bewail the loss of this rusty-red rail?
It was a long-necked, long-beaked, long-legged hen.
In the home of the dodo, they flocked like quail
and covered the island until Portuguese seamen

and Dutch in the 1500s set sail,
visiting islands unexplored before then.
Why bewail the loss of this rusty-red rail?
Just a long-necked, long-beaked, long-legged hen,

flightless, attracted to red (cap or rag) runs the tale;
they were easily caught, and the squawks would bring ten
more to be beaten and killed by the men
until none left but bones, drawings, and written portrayal.
I bewail the loss of this rusty-red rail.

RHONDEAU FOR THE RODRIGUEZ SOLITAIRE

A bird of beauty rare with craws like breasts
where feathers whiter were and bosoms dressed.
Their dances graced displays with wing tips knobbed
that rattled, clapped, and whirred the short wings bobbed.
Their long and slender necks rose from their chest.

Mating for life like other doves that nest
with but one chick, they fed and cared obsessed
and drove away all others. When caught, they sobbed,
a bird of beauty rare.

Their slender beaks, a widow's peak, moustache
of darker brown adorned their face and pressed
above their nostrils prettily and daubed
a darker line around their eyes. We're robbed
because they were as lovely to the taste,
a bird of beauty rare.

PANTOUM FOR THE PIGEON HOLLANDAISE

The pigeon hollandaise was colored deep blue,
a deep marine blue with a hot pepper tail,
and a scarlet ellipse around its eye too,
with white crest and breast like a hood of chain mail.

A deep marine blue with a hot pepper tail,
as delicious to eat as it was to behold,
with its white crest and breast like a hood of chain mail,
its white beak was tipped with a coin of gold.

As delicious to eat as it was to behold,
its feet were red, but a butter-sauced yellow
tipped its white beak with a coin of gold.
Oh, this graceful bird was a tropical fellow!

Its feet were red, but a butter-sauced yellow
attracted the hunters, cats, dogs, other pests.
Oh, this graceful bird was a tropical fellow,
but it was the pet monkeys that raided the nests.

It wasn't the hunters, cats, dogs, other pests
that came to live on Mauritius Island,
but it was the pet monkeys that raided the nests,
that killed off the very last specimen.

When men came to live on Mauritius Island,
and then ceased to see the red-circled eye, too,
they were blind to the death of the very last specimen
of the pigeon hollandaise colored deep blue.

SESTINA FOR THE STEPHENS ISLAND WREN

Not far from New Zealand's South Island
lies a small wooded island named Stephens.
It once was the home of wee wrens
that were cute little birds with fanned wings
as big as their bodies, and tails moth-like
cut short to roll in your palm, but a cat--

Yes, it was but one solitary cat
that came to this secluded island
with a lighthouse keeper, and like
he'd brought snakes to slither over Stephens,
this cat caught all those birds with weak wings
as they scurried at night. These rare wrens

ran more like young mice than like wrens,
and they lived in rock holes, so the cat
could easy catch those who took wing
while he freely explored the whole island.
Like a cougar chasing chicks, he roamed Stephens.
The keeper and collectors all alike

watched and reported on these birds so unlike
other species of birds and small wrens
from the lands across oceans from Stephens
where birds can fly fast from a cat.
Such predators were unknown to this island.
Birds had simply no need for strong wings.

On South Island lived birds with no wings
peculiar to only New Zealand, much like
the moas, all killed when men came to the island.

It was less than a year for the wrens
to become all extinct by this cat
that was brought to the lighthouse on Stephens.

As the mob that threw stones at Saint Stephen
blindly watched as his spirit took wing,
Saul crouched with his eyes like a cat
but was scared on the road so much like
the timid and meek little wrens
that disappeared in one year from that island.

Why did those men who came to that island called Stephens
and discovered unknown wrens with weak wings and then let
them all be killed and brought to them like mice by their cat?

Stephens Island Wrens
Beverley-Rose Enright

RUBAIYAT FOR INDIA'S PINK-HEADED DUCK

North of the Ganges and west Brahmaputra,
Wings whistling softly, the drake's mellow "waugh-uh"
Mid the loud quacking in ponds and in lakes,
Grasslands and floodplains, with crocs and with *tigras*.

Humans did hunt these ducks all the year, taking
Just fifty years to drop abundant drakes
Down to but ten that can't breed in a park
Far off in England from their swampy brake.

A rosy-pink head was its distinctive mark,
And it laid global eggs, moon-white balls in the dark;
Shell pink under wings and its bill brightly pink,
Long neck was its crescent moon's vanishing arc.

LAMENT FOR THE LABRADOR DUCK

It was a North Atlantic duck,
Native to New England and New York.
It's said to have summered in Labrador
And nested on islands in Saint Lawrence
And wintered on coasts south to Long Island.

Lost in the Labrador Sea.

The male, white-headed and white-winged,
Had a black body and black-collared neck
With a black stripe on top of its head
Lined up like a mohawk haircut.

Lost in the Labrador Sea.

The beak was orange and especially shaped
For eating mussels and other shellfish.
Colored brown were the female and immature ducks.

Lost in the Labrador Sea.

Shot like other ducks, they tasted fishy.
They were seldom seen or eaten either.

Lost in the Labrador Sea.

The male ducks were first to disappear
Because of feather hunters and collectors.
Marine museums have a stuffed few.
Artists have drawn and painted for us to view
This most uniquely distinctive duck.

Lost in the Labrador Sea.

Labrador Duck
Beverley Rose Enright

VILLANELLE FOR THE PAINTED VULTURE

The painted vulture's wings and tail were white
with brown; its long soft ruff could hide its head.
The natives used wing quills to make peace-pipes.

The bare skin of the head and neck had stripes
of loosely wrinkled purple, yellow, red.
The colors sparked the wings' and tail's white.

The stomach hung, a pouch of reddish light
until it bulged from roasted reptiles fed.
The natives used wing quills to make peace pipes.

It had white legs and feet, a yellow bill fit tight
from the purple cheeks beneath the crown of red.
The painted vulture's wings and tail were white.

When fires flamed the Florida meadows bright,
flocks of these vultures searched for burning dead
snakes, lizards, leaving quills to make peace pipes.

The eighteenth-century's Florida frosts did smite
severely the white tender toes, and spread
these perished vultures' wings and tails so white
the natives used wing quills to make peace pipes.

BLUES FOR BRACE'S EMERALD HUMMINGBIRD

You know a hummingbird is a bird that hums.
Yep, a hummingbird's a bird that hums,
an electric guitar as big as your thumb.

But a hummingbird's not a bird that sings.
I say a hummingbird's not a bird that sings.
That sound he makes is his whirring wings.

Well, a hummingbird is a bird so small;
Yep, a hummingbird is a bird so small,
it sips the nectar through a syringe-like straw.

Man, this hummingbird is colored bright.
I say this hummingbird is neon bright,
a living jewel shot through with light.

Well, this emerald bird's without a sound.
You know this emerald bird's no longer around.
The stuffed one's the same as the fossils found.

Oh, it's niche was so small in the 1800's;
I say it's numbers so little as the 1800's
closed, it dropped to zero numbers.

Well, Lewis Brace found just this one bird.
I say Lewis Brace found this now-stuffed bird.
That's why we know, and how we heard.

But I wonder if we could have saved those lives,
and turned a relict bird into one that thrives.

HAIKU FOR THE RYUKYU KINGFISHER

Wings of peacock jade
send a flaming scarlet spear
deep into the sea.

HEROIC COUPLETS FOR THE HEATH HEN

They bred and fed in groups one-thousand strong
or more; in spring the male birds in mating's song
"boomed" out noisily their dance and strut,
displaying to female birds their fan-ringed butts
with flaring feathers and bright orange-swelled necks,
a giant mass of troops entreating sex.
When early settlers to New England found
them everywhere upon the brushy ground
of Boston, they were shot so constantly
that servants were told by cooks to see
that heath hen was not on the table everyday,
but only a few times a week. To slay
so many birds so fast, the numbers fell
quite quickly. The Long Islanders proposed a bill
for a closed season to preserve heath hen.
But when the Act was read, the members said
they could not see the reason, as they misread,
"for preserving Indians or other heathen."
The over-hunting did but partly threaten
the heath hen's dwindling numbers, their ground nests
made them vulnerable to many pests.
Dogs, cats, and rats, new predators, disease
from old-world chickens, pheasants, seized
in epidemics native birds, and then
the final blow to end their kind came when
the prairie was converted into farmland.
By eighteen-thirty none lived on the mainland,
but still were found in Martha's Vineyard Island
in Massachusetts; a small band
of birds grew smaller yet, falling to less
than fifty when a reservation, yes,

sixteen-hundred acres was set up,
and numbers did a two-thousand higher jump.
But then in nineteen-sixteen came a fire
that burned the breeding area entire.
It was followed by a winter so severe,
that but one hundred-fifty birds lived there.
And then blackhead disease brought in by turkeys
reduced the number down to but thirteen
that further fell to two, and nineteen-thirty
did see just one heath hen that narrowly
escaped a passing car delaying fate
just two more years, because without a mate
the heath hen joined the company of birds
that passed into extinction from great herds.

A BALLAD FOR THE AMERICAN IVORY-BILLED WOODPECKER

Vast timberlands throughout the South
    Can no more be found.
That's why this giant woodpecker
    No longer makes a sound.

The loss of habitat's not all
    That made it disappear.
Hunters and collectors too
    Make us shed a tear.

A striking twenty inches long
    "Van Dyck" to Audubon,
Four-hundred specimens exist
    Although the bird is gone.

The Indians made necklaces
    And crowns of the ivory bills,
White-wing feathered headdresses
    With red-crest feathered frills.

Alexander Wilson wrote
    That once he wounded one
And kept it in his hotel room
    While he cared for his roan.

When he returned into his room
    The bird made such a shout
Of grief because the man had caught
    It trying to get out.

The bird had pecked into the wall
    Near where the ceiling starts
Exposing fifteen inches square
    Of lath and plaster parts.

A fist-wide hole had been pecked through
    Into the weatherboard.
One hour more it would have reached
    What it was pecking toward.

Though wounded it would get away
    But that was not to be.
It'd been discovered and it screamed
    In all its heart and beauty.

Each pair of birds needed a spread
    Two-thousand acres wide
Of mature river bottom forest
    To live and breed and hide.

Vast timberlands throughout the South
    Can no more be found.
That's why this giant woodpecker
    No longer makes a sound.

SEXTILLA FOR THE IMPERIAL WOODPECKER OF THE MEXICAN SIERRA MADRE

It was the largest woodpecker
of all time. Men were the wrecker
of its line. Indians to get
the tasty young from tall trees, felled
the sixty-two foot pines that held
woodpecker nests with no regret.

DOUBLE FIVE* FOR THE DELALANDE'S COUCAL

The hope the snail-eating *coua
delalandei* still survives
is very slim. The last
definite record comes from 1834,
but rumors circle and don't die.

Rumors circle that the birds still lived
in the 1920s, rare and shy,
deep in the rain forest, but no,
no reports were ever confirmed. Only
was it certain they lived on Ile de Saint-Marie.

Rumors circle that they lived and maybe still
live on nearby Madagascar, but again
no reports confirmed. The original forest
habitat is gone, long gone. Long gone the blue,
ultramarine-blue feathers spread

over the wings, back, and head,
around the eye, and the tail blue-green
feathers tipped with white, and white
flowed down the throat and neck,
and down the breast to a chestnut abdomen

and upper legs; the feet and beak charcoal.
Stuffed specimens of this large lost bird,
twenty-two inches long, are just thirteen,
in London, Paris, Liverpool, Philadelphia, New York,
Cambridge, Brussels, Vienna, Tananarive, Stuttgart.

*form often used by Philip Dacey

A LIMERICK FOR THE LAUGHING OWL

There once were large owls in New Zealand,
Whekaus of the North and South Islands.
    They chuckled, they cooed,
    They whistled, they mewed,
Hysterically laughed as they left with their woodlands.

Laughing owl
Beverley Rose Enright

FUGUE FOR FORSTER'S TANNA DOVE

South of the Solomon Islands,
East on the rim of the Coral Sea,
Is an island the natives named Tanna
Found in the New Hebrides.

Captain James Cook anchored his sloops
South of the Solomon Islands
After circling an island named Tanna
Measuring twenty-five leagues.

On Tanna was an active volcano
Found on the rim of the Coral Sea,
Far from the harbor with hot springs named Doogos
Where Captain Cook anchored his sloops.

On one sloop was the naturalist Forster
Investigating with his illustrator son
The birds and the plants found on Tanna,
An island in the New Hebrides.

In the center was an active volcano
Spewing a cauliflower-shaped cloud
And hot springs named Doogos ascended
Close to the harbor's tide line.

In a wood on the island named Tanna
Forster shot a new species of bird
And found in its craw a nutmeg
While investigating 'round near the Doogos.

South of the Solomon Islands
On an island east of the Coral Sea,
A new species of dove named the Tanna
Was painted by Forster's artist son.

A small dove was found on an island
Named Tanna in the New Hebrides
With a rusty-brown head, breast, and red feet,
Gray belly, black bill, dark green wings.

This new species of dove was named Tanna
Eating fruits of the trees in the wood
On a volcano made island and hot springs
Near the harbor where Captain Cook docked his sloops.

The dove now named Tanna had red feet,
Grey belly, and red-purple back
With a rusty red breast and dark green wings
Painted by Forster's artist son.

Inside twenty-five leagues that circled
The island the natives named Tanna
Was discovered a new species of dove
Made extinct twenty years after.

Forster's description and his son's artistry
Are all that remain of this very rare species
Once found on an island named Tanna
In a wood where grew nutmeg trees.

East on the rim of the Coral Sea
Was a bird on Tanna Island, red, purple, and green,
A dove painted and described by the Forsters
Forever lost from the New Hebrides.

SEGUIDILLA FOR THE SAINT KITTS PUERTO RICAN BULLFINCH

The "mountain blacksmith" sings
   like cardinals trill
in seven notes that spring
   from a big bill
where tiny hammers ring
   a silver anvil.
   The monkeys wrest
the red head and black wings
   and rob the nest.

RUBLIW* FOR THE MARQUESAS FRUIT DOVE

Dear dove,
you lived above
the canopy whereof
the islands in the middle shove
the South Pacific Ocean's global glove.
A red moustached blue head, olive
covered the feathers of
your wings above
with love.

*form invented by Richard Wilbur

OCTAVA RIMA ODE ON THE HAWAIIAN ISLANDS ʻOʻOS

I.

Very distinctive was the call of the ʻoʻo:
ow-ow, ow-ow, ow,! A shout, a shout, a shriek!
could be heard from the bird no matter how
high was its forest perch or mountain peak.
It could sound hoarse in some ʻoʻos, or the vowel
could be flute-like on Kauai; each species was unique
to Oahu, Hawaii, Molokai, and Kauai habitats
before the arrival of cattle, pigs, goats, cats, and rats.

II.

Plumage differed also on anʻoʻo from each island.
Oahu ʻoʻos had long chevroned tails in white and black.
Hawaii ʻoʻos were trapped to fill the demands
for the orange feathers and yellow tufts plucked
to make royal robes and capes woven of thousands
of feathers from birds that were not released back
to their forests, but eagerly fried in their fat.
Molokai ʻoʻos had yellow tuft cheeks neath metallic hats.

III.

These magnificent ʻoʻos were not immune to disease,
the avian malaria from foreign mosquitoes
brought to the islands by Europeans across seas.
Their cats were seen devouring dozens of ʻoʻos;
their rats were seen running in daylight up trees.
Their cattle trampled bushes. Settlers used saws and hoes.
These islands are in danger of becoming desert, some suppose,
and almost all the native birds are extinct like the ʻoʻos.

Oahu 'O'o
Beverley Rose Enright

PUSHKIN SONNET FOR THE LAYSAN MILLERBIRD

Laysan is an outer island in Hawaii.
The millerbird that lived there was a warbler,
blest with a song as liquid as the sea,
as full of melody as a happy bugler.

It's favorite food was moths that were named "millers",
and especially they liked the caterpillars.
They were so tame they'd land on a person's head,
and flocks showed up at meals to be fed.

But that was early on in nineteen-thirteen,
the year the rabbits were brought to the island
that soon became a barren waste of sand.

Such a desert that the lake's bright sheen
seemed a mirage, for all the life was gone;
despondent whispers replaced the lost song.

GOLDEN SECTION THIRTEENER FOR THE GUADELOUPE AMAZON

Hen-sized parrots that had a duck-like flight,
    they lived on a small island.
Their iridescent purple feathers bright,
    a red, green, yellow blend,
the "roses" on the wings, a striking sight,

and red around the eyes, black beak and feet,
    attracted merchants, slaves,
and settlers clearing forests, hunting meat,
    for no bird-lover staves
the slaughter, loss of forests that complete
    the wipeout no one saves.
No island paradise could long escape
the tropics' spread of slave plantation's rape.

A CHANT FOR THE CHATHAM ISLAND BELLBIRD (MAKO MAKO)

Men wrote of bird concerts when they came to Chatham Island.
Men wrote after they arrived and awakened ashore.
Men wrote of hearing a heavenly heralding.
Men wrote of singing sounding like small silver bells.
Men wrote that they named the once numerous bellbirds.
Men wrote of the mako mako's memorable chimes.
Men wrote of the blue heads and bluish green bodies.
Men wrote of the shooting and selling of stuffed skins.
Men wrote of seeing the singers they still sought no more.

BLACK CAULDRON ANTHEM FOR THE GREAT AUK

Thousands of thousands and ten times thousands
Which no man could number over the islands
In the North Atlantic and especially Funk Island
Where they brought the great black cauldron.

Thousands of thousands of black-headed penguins
Were stunned and grabbed and cast
Into the boiling brine for to gather
Thousands of thousands of pounds of feathers.

The naked dead fed the fire and thousands
Of thousands were tossed on the sand
To slide into the sea with the tides.
Mercy, mercy, I sigh, but there was none.

We still have ducks and geese, and yet
Why kill all the great auks for feather beds?
Why not let some still live and be?
They decomposed eternally in the sea.

I ask those men who killed that last breeding pair,
Who stomped the egg, oh why oh why oh why
Did cruel fate lead them there? Why the heel?
Why the hate? Why the urge to exterminate?

Auk, auk, auk, and when one last stuffed auk
Brought the highest price ever paid at auction
For a stuffed bird specimen, I question:
What was the threat? What was the fear?
Is there regret? Is there a tear?

Great Auk

TWIN TRIOLETS FOR THE CAROLINA PARAKEET

There were so many in the woods
And in the orchards that came after
That angry farmers shot the floods.
There were so many in the woods
Of yellow green sparked with orange hoods,
They killed entire flocks in laughter.
There were so many in the woods
And in the orchards that came after.

We look at the stuffed birds and brood
On beauty lost forever after.
They fed on grain and orchard foods.
We look at the stuffed birds and brood
How nuisance numbers of winged roods
Provoked fate's fatal human grafter.
We look at the stuffed birds and brood
On beauty lost forever after.

CURTAL SONNET* FOR THE ESKIMO CURLEW

Audubon's prescient watercolor print
   Illustrates two Eskimo curlews.
      One lies dead or fatally injured.
The other curlew eyes it with a hint
   Of a question, is it just in a snooze,
      Or a forever dead bird.

Curlews once migrated in a massive flock
   From Alaska to Argentina and back, whose
      Seasonal flight pattern sadly ensured
Intense human hunting, a relentless stalk
      To end as pictured.

*form invented by Gerard Manley Hopkins

Sketch of a picture of a painting by John J. Audubon of two Eskimo Curlews
Beverley Rose Enright

PASSING AWAY STANZA FOR THE PASSENGER PIGEON

Flocks of two hundred million each
 once blocked the sun.
Flocks of two hundred million each
 were gunned to none.

A PARABLE FOR THE PARADISE PARROT

The kingdom of heaven is like unto
a pair of paradise parrots.
Their plumage was like unto a rainbow
come down to embrace a tree branch.
Red, yellow, chartreuse, and olive,
turquoise and blue eye-rings and feathers
on head, body, wings, tail, brightened
over the brown and the gray.
The male chirped softly and sweetly to his mate,
and his long mating call charmed her
with a force so intense it vibrated
all through his whole body and long tail.
You won't find these parrots
anywhere on this earth.
They are gone from the wild
and gone even from the cages,
for Europeans brought two centuries ago
their cats, rats, and foxes, their cattle and sheep,
to those homes in the termite mounds,
to the holes in steep riverbanks,
to those feeding grounds in Queensland,
to that habitat in the Darling Downs.
Put a pair of these parrots
from the paintings and pages in books,
into your mind and into your heart,
and the paradise of heaven is within you.

TRIOLETS OF TENDERNESS

OUR NATIONAL SYMBOL WAS ALMOST LOST

Once the bald eagle was endangered,
for DDT made it almost extinct.
Biologists researched and spread the word
why the bald eagle was endangered,
and it was brought back from the brink
when DDT was banned and saved the bird.
Once the bald eagle was endangered,
for DDT made it almost extinct.

MOTHER'S DAY AT LOMBARD'S LILACIA PARK

My son visits me at Lilacia Park.
He's a gifted man I seldom see.
So each lilac and tulip and sweet remark
when my son visits me at Lilacia Park
still sparkles in my memory
and planes the roughness of my life's bark.
My son visits me. At Lilacia Park
he's this gifted man I seldom see.

ARCHANGEL WITH THE GOLDEN HAIR

This angel haloed with gold hair
in braided curls around her face
shines with peace and loving care.
This angel haloed with gold hair
has large dark eyes that softly stare
straight deep into your wounded place,
this angel haloed with gold hair
in braided curls around her face.

NUTMEG

Beloved bunny, spice furred lop,
velvet pet, we're so heartbroken.
No more we'll watch you joyful hop,
beloved bunny, spice furred lop.
Blocked belly made your short life stop.
Honey-natured, smart, housebroken,
beloved bunny, spice furred lop,
velvet pet, we're so heartbroken.

Nutmeg — Beverley Rose Enright

YOUR HANDS

I love to see you move your hands
like couples dancing to your words
that every heartbeat understands.
I love to see you move your hands
like caravans caress the sands,
like brushstrokes or a flight of birds.
I love to see you move your hands
like couples dancing to your words.

JUST TO HOLD YOUR HAND

To lock your fingers into mine
or roll my fingers round your thumb
would pulse electric shock sublime.
To lock your fingers into mine
and squeeze, then finger your lifeline
would sock my soul a rush like rum.
Come, lock your fingers into mine
and roll our fingers round your thumb.

WHAT A COMFORT WAS YOUR VOICE

A voice soft as chiffon
As sweet as brandied butter
Melting like spring snow on the lawn
A voice soft as chiffon
The camouflage of a hiding fawn
The murmur of a wooing mutter
A voice soft as chiffon
As sweet as brandied butter

WITHOUT YOUR GLASSES

My love, your eyes look softer now
etched round by decades' tiny lines
without your glasses beneath your brow.
My love, your eyes look softer now,
becoming like a blooming bough,
feathered and fuzzy valentines.
My love, your eyes look softer now
etched round by decades' tiny lines.

"THE VOICE OF MY BELOVED, BEHOLD HE COMETH LEAPING"

His cello voice has a country sound,
faint echoes of West Virginia hills
where leaping rabbits and deer abound.
His cello voice has a country sound,
square dancers twirl as feet pound
and bluegrass fiddlers' music trills.
His cello voice has a country sound,
faint echoes of West Virginia hills.

THE VOICE OF LEAVES

He speaks the voice of leaves,
a crisp and rustling sound,
that whispers to the breeze.
He speaks the voice of leaves
to salve each one who grieves
for what is in the ground.
He speaks the voice of leaves,
a crisp and rustling sound.

MISTER RIGHT

> *In the thirtieth year of life*
> *I took my heart to be my wife.*
> J. V. Cunningham, "In the Thirtieth Year"

I asked my heart to be my husband.
My heart replied, "Of course, I do.
I am the source and force within." when
I asked my heart to be my husband.
All men I gave the keys would lose them,
Leave me still locked, without a clue.
I asked my heart to be my husband.
My heart replied, "Of course. I do."

ROMANTIC FEELINGS AND FANTASIES

FOUR LIEDER BY PHILIP KOPLOW

The following four songs
are from *Lucky Icons* and were chosen
by composer Philip Koplow
to set to music.
However, he passed on
to the next life after
a decade of fighting cancer
before he could complete the music
for the fourth song.

SPRING BIRD BLUES

Song Sparrows,
Spare me your songs;
This wrong is past mending.

Mourning Doves,
Moan in the morning;
I mourn with each new daffodil.

Red-breasted Robins,
Go cheer up the rain;
This breast burns red with pain.

Chattering Blue Jays,
Flash feathers and fly;
Bluer than you flow my days.

DANCING SONG

I'm dancing away to the sunset
   clothed in red velvet and pearls.
I'm dancing away in the twilight.
    Come, take my hand as we twirl.

I'm dancing away in the starshine
   clothed in transparent blue veils.
I'm dancing away in the moonlight
   that shines on my silvery curls.

I'm dancing away in the darkness
   clothed in black velvet and night.
I'm dancing away to the distance.
   I'm dancing away out of sight.

MY SONG WAS GONE

Yesterday
my song was gone.
All I could do was pray.

Yesterday
my mood unglued,
and all around was gray.

Yesterday
my eyes were sighs
that would not go away.

But all of that was yesterday.

Now today
I heard the birds
and saw a rose bouquet.

Now today
my heart's Mozart
as light as orange soufflé.

Now today
I feel ideal,
and life's a free buffet,

for I dreamed you loved me today.

THE SEA OF LOVE

There is a long unconscious sea
that ebbs and flows continuously
in all of us and especially
through you and me.

While some pollute the water's mirror,
a heavenly presence makes it clear
and clean so we can persevere,
and no poison fear.

I send this loving message through
to help make every dream come true
and wash each pain with honeydew.
May God bless you.

APPLES

To get apples
you need two apple trees.
Just one won't do.
And bees.
It could be as few
as one or two
or more like three or four
or five
or a whole hive.

For love poetry
you need two
the lover and beloved
and another sort of bee
chemistry.

THE ANGEL WITH THE FLAMING DART

Saint Theresa tells
a thrilling tale
of an episode
of ecstasy
that came to her exploding
climactically
from being spiritually pierced,
speared by an angel.
Me, too.
and not just once or twice
but many times.
as if the air were sparked,
electric with these invisible angels
and their fiery darts.
I wonder where they come from.
Body chemistry?
Psychic energy?
Beats me.

THE PRINCE

Once upon a time
when I was a college student
living in a dormitory
with two loving roommates,
I was buzzed by the main desk
telling me I had a visitor.
And standing there
was a handsome prince.
Well, he looked that way
to me that day, but soon
a classmate walked in
to see me too, but looked
and took to him
like an offering of chocolate mints.
And the prince walked out the door
with her and became her male friend
(who turned out to be homosexual).
My roommates watched it all
from the third-floor dorm window
and were upset and angry at her.
But I was not because I thought
what did it matter
or mean to me since
he was free
to not be my prince
and I was free
of the fairy tale.
It was a slender clear glass vase
of five viridian rose stems
with five invisible roses.

THIS TOO WILL PASS

The recurring memory of that shocking sight,
My old friend standing naked in white briefs,
Burns through my every day and every night.

In a library once sat he with a white
Handkerchief tucked between his thighs, motif,
A recurring memory of a curious sight.

Such fond images from fifty years ignite
And resonate like flaming bas relief
Burns through my every day and every night.

And once he spent a New Year's Eve, polite
And earnest, stating his civilized beliefs,
A recurring memory of an endearing sight.

In vain, I wheel my crippled will contrite,
In vain, I would forget his form, this grief
Burns through my every day and every night.

I wish that in his artful script he'd write,
My old friend standing naked in white briefs.
The recurring memory of that shocking sight
Burns through my every day and every night.

BREAKFAST

After I dreamed of wanting him
who was not mine to have,
I stacked my silly wishes, whims,
like pancakes on a plate,
and felt my knife of reason cut
and fork of knowledge pierce
every morsel of sad fate I ate.

When I poured my heated passions,
hot maple syrup melting butter
of mistake with every bite,
I did partake a bitter tablespoon
of stern reproof and soured cream
of real-life correction
to wipe away from mouth and mind
smears and streams of foolish dreams.

But blueberries of blessings
and cantaloupes of caring thoughts
spooned into a bowl of cheerful cherries
brought me to a recollection
of what succors and sustains,
thoughts that hum with honey makers
sweeten lemons in the juice
of noose and crucifixion, sating
with a smile to stun
the sun to fun.

ONLY A FANTASY

You could come to Chicago.
We could go to an opera,
But it's only a fantasy.
I could take the train.
You could take a cab,
But it's just not meant to be.

I could go to New York.
We could meet at the Met,
But it's only a fantasy.
I could drive there or fly.
You could get a chauffeur,
But that too, is not to be.

We could meet up in Cleveland,
And go to the zoo,
But it's only a fantasy;
Perhaps one of your shows,
And the Art Museum too,
But that can never be.

We could sit near each other
Like sister and brother,
But that's only a fantasy;
Or even be lovers
Until it's all over,
But it's best to be Emily D.

FANCIFUL DIALOGUE FOR WHEN WE FIRST MEET

He: Oh, do not be afraid of me, my dear.
    Surely by now we know each other's soul;
    and though our body's form may strange appear,
    our love will speed us quickly to our goal.

She: But not too fast so that the inner light
    has time to cast its glow upon our faces
    and lift the mask of strangeness from our sight
    so we in comfort make our fond embraces.

He: Then let me hold your hand and let me touch
    your fingers to my lips and closer move.
    We've waited long to hesitate this much.

She: But still restraint will ease our fears and soothe

He: Your smile shines through the mask; I only see
    The vision that you painted deep within me.

YOU COME TO ME IN THE NIGHT

In the day you are distant
    Or that's what it seems,
But at night you come to me
    With love in my dreams.

In the day I see license plates
    That have your initial,
But at night your dear name
    Sounds uniquely special.

In the day I'm forgetful
    Of people I once knew,
But at night there is only
    For me thoughts of you.

In the day I can't see you
    For all of my wishes;
But at night, O my dear love,
    You cover me with kisses.

In the day there's no letter
    From you in the mail,
But at night when I slumber,
    You're a romantic tale.

In the day you're far from me
    Or that's what it seems,
But at night you embrace me
    With love in my dreams.

TELEPATHY

Kiss my lips and press me tight
as if it were our wedding night;
and though we sleep in distant beds,
we send the pictures through our heads,
and our bodies feel the touch
as though we actually could clutch
our flesh and such.

Hold your hand upon my breast,
and let our passion do the rest;
though we're a thousand miles apart,
we send the feeling through the heart,
and our bodies thrill as though
we lie together in the glow
of mutual love.

WILD HORSES

could not drag me away from you
for the number of mustangs on the range are few
because men corral and reduce the herd
and reduce the land where they can run free
so it seems the plan is to make a preserve
which seems to me rather like creating a zoo
where buses of visitors drive on through
and the range must be small to keep some in view.
Whatever you want and whatever I do,
wild horses can't drag me away from you.

YOUR FACE

I saw your face as
   a dream serene
Like a snowfall graces
   a winter's scene.

I saw your face in
   a halo of white
Hair and like frost in
   a beard of light.

I saw your face lined
   like November trees,
An etching designed
   and traced with skis.

I saw your face so
   seasoned with years
Falling soft and slow
   like snowflake tears.

I saw your face as
   a winter's dream
When snow embraces
   a symphonic theme.

PARADELLE* OF PAST LOVE

Your love flies and dies on the pines.
Your love flies and dies on the pines
As the frog leaps like bread from the toaster,
As the frog leaps like bread from the toaster.
The frog pines and dies as the flies
Like love leaps on the bread from your toaster.

I wish that my dreams end in waterfalls.
I wish that my dreams end in waterfalls.
The foam fills the sponges in the sink.
The foam fills the sponges in the sink.
My dreams sink in foam in the sponges.
The end that I wish fills the waterfalls.

Your face burns the lamplight of memories.
Your face burns the lamplight of memories.
The leaves bleed their red on the mums.
The leaves bleed their red on the mums.
Your mums face the bleed of the memories
The red lamplight burns on their leaves.

Mums the end of the dreams on memories.
My love pines and dies in their waterfalls
That leaves the red bleed on your face.
The lamplight leaps the frog, the wish flies.
The bread burns from your toaster like the foam
Fills in the sponges as I sink.

*form invented by Billy Collins

PARADELLE OF SPENT PASSION

I remember the spark that you sent me.
I remember the spark that you sent me.
It was a reply in the post.
It was a reply in the post.
In the post you sent me a reply.
It was the spark that I remember.

My emotions unrolled like a flag.
My emotions unrolled like a flag
Flutters its colors in the sunshine,
Flutters its colors in the sunshine.
My flag colors like the unrolled emotions
A sun flutters in its shine.

I soared and then settled in the silence.
I soared and then settled in the silence
That troubled me until you wrote again,
That troubled me until you wrote again.
The troubled silence settled me until
I wrote you and then soared again.

I remember I wrote you and soared
Like the colors shine in the sun,
Until in the reply that you sent me
Was a spark that unrolled a flag post.
Its silence again troubled my flutters,
Then it settled the emotions in me.

RED GLASS

At the Ron-Day-Voo,
a bar near Kent State U,
the light blinks red
in rhodochrosite shadows,
vermilion blacks.
I see you come in, and you sit down
across from me, lit up in red,
so fitting since you are a Red.
Though I know why
I did not warm to Marx or Trotsky.
It was the part of you that once
loved Jesus Christ as passionately
as you love those commies now
that made me burn in our bonfire
of unresolved tension.
But all your arguments
could not move me any further left
than the Christian
Democratic Socialist utopia.
We were two virgins
and you wanted it to go
a way I could not go
without the blessing of the church.
The tension burned to molten glass,
the green-stemmed wineglass
that held the *rose* of our love,
and then you snapped and broke it.
The wine fire cooled on shattered shards.
It cut my hands to pick them up
to throw at you.
It cut my hands, it cut my heart,

and I lay for days with the stabbing.
There is a bridge
that we stood on
over the Cuyahoga river
where we held hands and kissed
and stared into the water.
At the Ron-Day-Voo
I stare at you
while the light blinks red
on your face mocking mine.
But what's all that to me?
A rood, a rhyme.

TRAIN WRECK

Our friendship has, alas, become a train wreck.
I wrack my brain for how to make it right.
The engine's on its side with the wheels spinning.
The boxcars are thrown off this way and that.
All are surrounded by a herd of moaning cattle.
On a tabletop I could pick up the pieces,
But this mess needs a hand like a jet airplane,
A jet airplane flying, bringing you to me.

IT'S OVER

Tears and fears,
fears and tears,
burning and churning,
turning and yearning,
waking and quaking,
shaking, heartbreaking,
longing for belonging,
reviewing the years,
over five decades,
that cloudy and clear.

Letters and looks,
fetters and books,
feelings and fancies,
fondness and friendship
flow through the years, tears
then dry with a sigh
over what's broken, unspoken,
wondering why.

WETNESS

Today I'll weep a little bit
and maybe more tomorrow,
even though I cannot see
a reason for the sorrow.

It's rather like the skin
of water on a glass
when cold inside meets warm outside
outlining a circled space,

or like a nervous sweaty hand
wet from the growing fear
that it will never hold your hand
or touch you standing near.

RAIN SONG

I love the muttering thunder
when lightning splits asunder
the black skies.

I love the splattering patter
of raindrops as they batter
and baptize.

I love the smell of moisture
in the soaked air cleaned and pure
as it dries.

I love when plants and flowers
drink up the drip of showers
as they rise.

I love you folding the umbrella,
a damp but smiling fella
with wet eyes.

AT LAKE PORTAGE IN CENTRAL MICHIGAN

I watch the water lick the shoreline
while seated on a bench.
It licks it like an open face
apple-butterscotch sandwich,
and the sand, which the water
kisses at the shore has liquid lips
touching tongues
in a thin line of foam.
The descending sun
shines a wide highway
across the lake that I
could not walk or drive
a car on, but need a boat.
Are we in the same boat?
You touched me twice a moment
on my side to gently guide
my way one day and I
so wanted you a moment or two
to gently put your arm
around my shoulder,
so I could lay my head
upon your shoulder,
and you could kiss my hair
like a breeze now gently strokes
the thinning threads.
The water laps and licks the shore
like apple butter spread
on a sandwich, the sand, which
licked by the lips
and tongues of the lake,
shadows the shine

of the hazardous highway
that crosses the lake
of my descending life's
foolish desires.

IF I WERE A BLOOMING LILAC BUSH

If I were a blooming lilac bush
and you were a wandering nose,
I would pull you close with my perfume,
and all through a long afternoon,
I would scent your drowsy doze.

If I were a Mozart string quartet
and you were a pair of loitering ears,
I would enchant your evening away
and cast a spell to make you stay
with music that echoes through years.

If I were a garden of many hued tulips
and you were a pair of roaming eyes,
I would capture and dazzle your sight
with my spectrum of colors delight
and brighten the drabbest of views.

If I were a warm breeze a-blowing
and you were a pair of idling feet,
I would whisk and spin you leaping
in rhythm to my swaying and sweeping
and whirl you waltzing down the street.

If I were and you were, alas, we are not,
for distance and silence have tied such a knot
that all our warm feelings have now come to naught.

But I cannot end this there, dead branches in despair,
when spring springs as it will with flowers fair
and lilacs bloom intense perfume to scent the air.

"I AM THE ROSE OF SHARON AND THE LILY OF THE VALLEY"

A Rose of Sharon blooms in your backyard
emailed in a photo, a type of hibiscus bush.
My middle name is Rose, but that is hard;
I'm fat, old, flabby now, and can't wear blush.

But I make quilts that bloom with beauty, starred
with roses appliquéd, and paintings brushed
in designs from an eighteenth-century postcard
named the Rose of Sharon from the Bible verse.

The lily of the valley, when a child I recall,
peeked between the folded blades of green,
white picot edged bonnets and bells, quite small
where trolls and elves and fairies dwelled unseen.

I love the flowers; though I no longer bloom,
I plant and sew to flower my yard and room.

Rose of Sharon appliqué quilt block pattern

adapted from an 1840 New England quilt
by Beverley Rose Enright

"THY LOVE IS BETTER THAN WINE"

I tiptoed through your mind you wrote to me,
so you were moved to compose a melody
swelling to a chorus of compliments,
enchanted legends of long-ago events,
shouting hallelujah in hyperbole.

All this intoxicating flattery
was way too much for this old heart to see
as simply what a longing mind invents
I tiptoed through.

What hidden springs of love this letter sent!
What generous joy, exploding sentiment
was in that heart and mind and memory
I tiptoed through.

"RISE UP, MY LOVE, MY FAIR ONE, AND COME AWAY"

Rise up, awake from your slumber.
Rise up from your soreness and pain.
Lift up the watery window
And see the sun's colors through the rain.

My love, four hundred miles from me,
My love, send an email to my heart,
Tell me stories that live in memory
Using your phone labeled smart.

My fair one, I now see in a photo,
My fair one, I last met in youth,
Will the changes the decades show
Reveal our souls' deeper truth?

Come away, and see me in Ohio,
Come away, when I return and greet
Old friends I visit yearly now solo,
To the art museum go when we meet.

"BE THOU LIKE A YOUNG HART UPON THE MOUNTAINS OF SPICES"

Be young
In heart, my friend
Upon the mountaintop
Where what was heard was seldom sung
And what was whispered there will now ascend
With incense, candle flame, and chants, and will not drop
Held back from sad despair by grace descending, rising up
To heaven there inside that heart of Christ within the silent prayer
Held back from sad despair by grace descending, rising up
With incense, candle flame, and chants, and will not drop
And what was whispered there will now ascend
Where what was heard was seldom sung
Upon the mountaintop
In heart, my friend
Be young

BEVERLEY ROSE ENRIGHT was born December 5, 1941 in Lodi, Ohio and spent her youth at her grandparent's home in East Akron, Ohio. She received a B. A. degree with honors from Kent State University and has taught mathematics for 20 years with the Chicago Public School system. She is retired and lives in Streamwood, Illinois.

About her first book of poetry *Lucky Icons,* one of her former professors, Dr. Robert Sumner Jackson, wrote these words for Amazon:

> A powerful exploration. That's what I say, from my present position of one of Beverley Enright's early life college teachers in the area we call literature.
>
> I see here some of the only poems I have ever seen representing the post-modern cultural style––even though the post-modern cultural style –– in my sense of the term –– began to come into human consciousness and culture about a hundred years ago.
>
> How is this shown in Beverley Enright's poems? I begin to explain by taking note of the organization of the whole book –– several "sets" of poems apparently coming from various periods of the writer's life represent various forms of interior life –– distinguished from each other, yet related and building on each other, especially the later ones building on the earlier. Most importantly, these various forms include not only the religious, the family, and other aspects of the intimate that are characteristic of the modern period –– but also a set that seems to build on all of the previous.
>
> During the modern period only the "objective" which for most moderns –– strangely –– includes mathematics inside of the so-called scientific –– was/is allowed to be considered "Truth."

Poetry occupied the "subjective" to be thrust into the outer darkness as mere sentiment or opinion — impossible to be regarded as part of the "exact" sciences. From the side of the scientific community that arrogance is fading away, as the word "truth" has long ago disappeared from the vocabulary of the most prestigious scientists — to be replaced by "fruitful", or "useful" or similar cognates. I think, for example, of Max Planck's famous remark "Science cannot solve the ultimate mystery of Nature. And it is because in the last analysis we ourselves are part of the mystery we are trying to solve." [as cited in Michio Kaku's Parallel Worlds, 2005, pp. 157-8]

It's taking longer in poetry. The prejudices are deeper. However, here in Beverley Enright's [book] we have a courageous example in those mysterious poems on the Calculus — and their living relationship maintained to the other mysteries found in the other sets of poems through the integrity of the writer.

Bravo, Beverley Enright

CPSIA information can be obtained
at www.ICGtesting.com
Printed in the USA
BVHW031927291119
565085BV00017B/45/P